TALES FROM THE RIVER

AN ANTHOLOGY OF RIVER LITERATURE

Stormbird Press

Cover photography: Tim Palmer
Cover design and typesetting: Stormbird Press.

National Library of Australia Cataloguing-in-Publication entry:
Mulvenna, Donna, 1965–Editor.
Tales from the River: An Anthology of River Literature
ISBN-13: 978-1-925856-02-6 (pbk)
ISBN-13: 978-1-925856-03-3 (ebk)
1. Nature | 2. Wilderness | 3. Rivers | 4. Conservation

Stormbird Press is an imprint of Wild Migration Limited. Stormbird
Press books may be ordered through booksellers or by contacting:
Stormbird Press
PO Box 73
Parndana, 5220
South Australia
www.stormbirdpress.com

*Every year millions of unsold books get pulped because they fail to
meet the inflated sales projections of publishers who swamp the
market with excess copies to buffer out sales stands. This practice
drowns out many other fine titles and creates huge levels of waste
and petroleum fuel consumption when unsold books are shipped
back from bookstores to be pulped. When paper degrades in a
landfill it releases methane, a greenhouse gas emission 23 times
more potent than carbon dioxide. Pulping books is an unacceptable
practice. Stormbird Press consciously prints our books 'on demand'
to conserve Earth's finite and precious resources. This way, we
know, every book printed finds a home that treasures it.*

Men may dam it and say that they have made a lake, but it will still be a river. It will keep its nature and bide its time, like a caged animal alert for the slightest opening. In time, it will have its way; the dam, like the ancient cliffs, will be carried away piecemeal in the currents.
—Wendell Berry, The Unforeseen Wilderness, 1991

CONTENTS

Foreword   ix

Preface   xi

Disclaimer   xvi

Introduction   1

POLAR FRESHWATER

Memories of Hockley Lake   7
Ron Melchiore

TEMPERATE UPLAND RIVERS

Growing Up With Rivers   27
Tim Palmer

Seven Rivers   47
Rob Carney

TEMPERATE COASTAL RIVERS

The Wild Atnarko River   61
Mary Woodbury

Let the River Run   73
Wes Ferguson

Kayaking Chile's Pascua River   87
Diana Saverin

Prodigal River   99
Rebecca Lawton

Paddling the Sewershed   111
Brice Particelli

When a River is a Person   132
Gary Wockner

Catfish Bend   137
Lisa Knopp

Upo Wetlands to Doyo Islet   158
Louise Duff

TEMPERATE FLOODPLAIN RIVERS

Three Water Stories   175
Anthony Birch

The Willamette   184
Kathleen Dean Moore

River of the Past   194
Conor Mihell

The Loner 208
James Roberts

Three Rivers 219
Karen Lloyd

Under the Shade of a Stringybark 241
Margi Prideaux

TROPICAL UPLAND RIVERS

Wilder Rivers—French Amazonia 255
Donna Mulvenna

TROPICAL FLOODPLAIN RIVERS

On the Negro River 275
José Truda Palazzo, Jr.

Deafened by Nature 287
Jessica Groenendijk

The Mother River of India 294
Mariellen Ward

ABOUT THIS BOOK

Contributing Authors 303
Rivers are Imperilled 315
An Invitation from the Publisher 318

FOREWORD

Water is fundamental to life on earth. One of the most valuable resources in the world, it is under grave threat. Our pressure to develop and feed a growing appetite often translates into actions that are putting pressure on water supplies. The draining of wetlands, deforestation, over-extraction of groundwater and increased pollution from agriculture and industry have all taken their toll. So many of the world's greatest rivers no longer reach the ocean.

I am delighted to contribute to this anthology which is a deeply personal account of first-hand journeys with rivers in countries across the world. I have been lucky to have travelled to corners of the world, to see this close relationship. In India, I have witnessed the close and spiritual connection people share with the mighty Ganga river. In China, I have seen how people, government and industry are coming together to protect the great rivers. As a child in Oslo, I saw the transformation of the once polluted Akerselva river. A lifeline for people in the city, protecting it inspired people to take action. Today, the river is an amazing oasis in the heart of the city.

It is when people connect personally with an issue, that change happens. And this is why I believe publications like this are so important. Each story conveys a powerful message – that we must save the rivers of this planet. Because it is only when we save our rivers, will we be able to protect what we love. Rivers are essential to human life. They ask for nothing more than our care and respect.

Erik Solheim,
Executive Director, UN Environment

PREFACE

Tales of the River began as a personal journey, intended to capture the experiences of paddling along wild rivers in a little known territory called French Guiana. In Guiana, the rivers are the lifeblood of the people—magic rivers that turn all near them to life.

Key to virtually every type of Guianese industrial process, including generating hydroelectricity for the European Space Station, the rivers also serve as transportation pathways where villagers traverse by motorised *pirogues* and dug-out canoes. These local people, who live along rivers including the Maroni and the Oyapock which delineate Guiana's national borders, fight to preserve wild rivers, a critical link in their subsistent chain of life. These people are not persons in the past, tourist stereotypes or a collection of outdated traditions, but people who exist in the same time and space as those in the modern world, the rivers influencing innumerable aspects of their culture and society.

As rivers change course across the terrain, they leave a visual history. Our human ancestors originated on riversides, and then once great civilisations prospered along the banks of major rivers such as the Tigris, Euphrates, Ganges and Nile, which connected, supported and nurtured communities of every kind.

For the indigenous peoples of Australia, water needs to flow through their story places—waterways and wetlands—to enable them to continue their ceremonial business, which is crucially important to them. The Lakota phrase 'Mní wičhóni', or 'Water is life', was the anthem chanted by 5,000 marchers during the struggle to stop the building of the Dakota Access Pipeline. For long years, the Lakota, the Blackfeet and the other first nations tribes possessed a knowledge of how to live within the restrictions of the limited water supply of the 'Great American desert' of North America. The Maori of New Zealand believe the rivers are protected by the Atua (God). Failure to respect tapu—ceremonial restriction which has been placed on parts of the river by a tohunga or priest—results in trouble, sickness, or even death. For me, came the recognition that some of the most important decisions I made, and the passions I pursued were generated when my senses were enriched by the river, a vital place of restoration where the mind clears.

With a new appreciation and love for rivers came the sad news that the animals and people they support are in trouble. Earth, particularly when viewed from space, is clearly a water planet, but we are not managing our impact on this essential life force well. Water, our collective inheritance, is declining to near-record lows.

Our rivers put at risk because mankind damages their habitat by removing their water, polluting their water, or simply preventing them from flowing through the landscape as they always have.

Each year the pressures on water resources escalate, their conservation becoming more arduous because people throughout the world have forgotten. Taken for granted in influential and wealthy parts of the world because it flows from a tap, water is seldom given the reverence it warrants as a precious resource. Many remain oblivious that one-third of the global population live under conditions of severe water scarcity at least one month of the year. Half a billion people in the world face severe water scarcity all year round. Some children don't know where the water they drink comes from, others drink water from dammed rivers or contaminated sources that make them sick. Where water is plentiful people have forgotten water shortages impact global food security, disrupt economies, and negatively affect all aspects of human life. Even today, 80 per cent of global wastewater is left untreated, containing everything from human waste to highly toxic industrial discharges

The UN's Educational, Scientific and Cultural Organisation (UNESCO) releases a major annual report about water. Since its first edition in 2003, the urgency increases. Global water use has increased by a factor of six over the past 100 years, and human demand for water is growing at a rate of one percent each year. River systems are the zone of Earth's highest biological diversity–and also of our most intense human activity. Freshwater biodiversity is in a state of crisis and freshwater species are more endangered than those on land.

Since the 1990s, water pollution has worsened in almost all rivers in Africa, Asia and Latin America. Nutrient, pathogens and chemicals are flowing into our waterways. The deterioration of water quality is expected to further escalate over the next decades.

Roughly two-thirds of the world's rivers have suffered harm from the 50,000 large dams built over the past century. Many of the world's great rivers—the Indus, the Colorado and the Yellow rivers—no longer reach the ocean, turning once-productive deltas into biological deserts.

Large dams devastate biological diversity by flooding land, fragmenting habitat, and isolating species, interrupting the exchange of nutrients between ecosystems and cutting off migration routes. They reduce water and sediment flows to downstream habitat, and change the nature of a river's estuary, where many of the world's fish species spawn.

Meanwhile, climate change is exacerbating flood and drought risks almost everywhere. Scientific studies indicate dams and reservoirs are globally significant sources of the greenhouse gases carbon dioxide and, in particular, responsible for almost a quarter of all human-caused methane emissions; an estimated 104 million tonnes of dam methane equivalent to four to five percent of all human-caused warming.

Human demand for water–agricultural, industrial and domestic–is tipping the scales. We are losing life forms that have the ability to nourish us, keep our water clean, produce breathable air and fertile soil, and ultimately make our planet the amazing place it is. By failing to protect our biological richness and diversity, we undercut the re-generative capacity of the Earth, and undermine a life force which creates conditions conducive to life.

How do we stop this? Where do we start?

By standing *together* on the bank of a river.

Donna Mulvenna and Margi Prideaux, 2018

The publisher gratefully acknowledges the generous contribution of the authors, who span the globe, towards the publication of this book. While efforts have been made to standardise basic typesetting, each chapter is faithfully presented as it was submitted–in British or US English.

INTRODUCTION

Rivers are like stories. They comprise a beginning, a middle, and an end. In a literal sense, they start somewhere, meander or flow through the landscape, then end their journey. They also carry the story construct through time. In the beginning they are formed as nature intended: wild rivers. In the middle, they do as they have done naturally for millennia, flow freely, nourish and sustain. Or they would if humankind didn't intervene. The ending depends on our commitment to make even simple changes. Even those headed for a sad ending—the Salween, La Plata, Danube, Rio Grande, Ganges, Murray-Darling, Indus, Nile, Yangtze and Mekong, can have their stories reversed if returned to our consciousness.

There is much about rivers in literature, from great writers including Melville, Thoreau and Hemingway. Memories, retold through story are worth defending, because they tell of where we came from, foretell of where we are going, and remind us the crystal-clear rivers of our childhoods are the way they should be.

The magic and essential nature of rivers are reflected through the stories rippling through the pages of this book. Like water, these poignant tales connect and bind us to each other. We read of a moose swimming towards a man in a small boat, its head rising out of a cold Canadian northern river, its body acting as a submerged iceberg. These cold waters have witnessed such communions for millennia. In Australia, we are transported into the ancestral past of a storyteller who revisits the water holes and ponds that flowed around the roots of eucalyptus trees used by his people to build bark canoes. His country speaks to him.

In the Amazon, three young children paddle a pirogue. 'The eldest child is steering the boat with a long *takari* pole, performed as confidently as a child peddling a little three-wheeled cart in a city park.' Pink dolphins share the waters with a *gaiola*, regularly sweeping by the boat in small groups, and in Peru a family of giant otters and deafening birdsong hint at how places around the world used to be. How they were meant to be.

We feel the anguish and pain in heartrending stories where a community fails to stop the construction of a dam that will back up nine miles of river, creating California's fourth largest reservoir, and drowning 100 miles of fluctuating shoreline. We float with another author through a city where the river is hidden by high walls from 'city streets filled with more fast-food chains, tire shops and carpet salesmen than you could ever want', its flow is choked with random appliances, tires and plastic shopping bags, scattered like 'lost leaves caught on branches and rocks'.

We are restored of joy and hope when a Diya is pushed into the current, watching as it 'clears a shoal and skims lightly along the glossy black surface of the Ganga, a tiny retreating light in the darkness, swept along by the currents of the mighty river', as the author takes part in an ancient tradition.

Without story, rivers can never be remembered as the wild places they were. Each written word creates new memories, restores memories, and reminds us that protecting water, as a vital resource, is only half the task. Our connection with these magical, living sinews gives meaning and purposefulness to our world.

Tales of the River is a collection of stories for everyone who loves rivers and the natural world, which is all of us, whether or not we consciously realise it.

POLAR FRESHWATER

Polar Freshwater ecoregions comprise entire high latitude
drainages; from the headwaters to mouth.

MEMORIES OF HOCKLEY LAKE

Ron Melchiore

I didn't hear a sound, but a sixth sense told me I wasn't alone. From my small aluminum boat, I pivoted around and focused my attention. The big head of a moose was swimming towards me. I knew that attached to that head, below the surface, was a massive body, much like a submerged iceberg. As it drew closer, I grew increasingly nervous as to the intent of my new friend. "What in the world are you doing out here in the middle of the lake?" I thought to myself.

On this warm, calm summer's night, I had cut the motor and was drifting lazily along on our pristine lake, contemplating nothing in particular. My routine after dinner was to head out in the boat. No destination required. The simple pleasure of being out on the water was the perfect way to end the day.

The clear, cold water body was accessed only by float plane. Imagine if you will, boarding a small float plane. From the vantage point of the air, for as far as the eye can see, you will gaze upon an aerial tapestry of multi-hued green forest intermingled with jutting rock formations, lowland bogs, and glistening lakes; the perfect habitat for wildlife and outdoor adventurer alike.

To this day, I still have no idea what that moose was thinking when it swam ever closer to me. Living as remote as we did, I took no chances and fired up the motor. I slowly engaged the throttle so as not to startle it and gave it some space. The moose, disappointed I wouldn't give it a lift, soon turned around and headed back to shore. The black flies were miserable that evening so perhaps going for a swim was a way to get some relief from the biting insects.

I've always held an affection for water whether ocean, lake, or river, and through the years I've been fortunate to enjoy time on all of these. But none was as special as our time in the wilderness of Hockley Lake. I'd like to share with you the treasured memories I enjoyed on my beloved lake.

∞

I vividly remember the thrill of arriving and setting up camp while we built our new home in late summer of 1999. Johanna and I spent any free time on the lake in our small aluminum boat or paddling our canoe. Although we worked hard that summer, we took time to explore our new water playground, and we stalked the creatures of the deep with rod and reel.

What a thrill when I pulled up my first trout from the depths! Spoken like a true fisherman, my arms and shoulders ached as I struggled for hours to pull in that mighty fish. The boat and I were dragged up the lake and then down, and even with the motor on full throttle, in reverse, I couldn't stop that fish from giving me its personal tour of the lake.

I finally got the 2-*pound* trout to the surface, where I rested and caught my breath.

Okay, maybe I embellished my fish tale a little, but it was a thrill to catch the first fish and to know fish were there. Lots of them. But until we caught that first trout, we were concerned we had just settled on the Dead Sea.

You might wonder how one gets an aluminum boat or canoe out into that wilderness setting. Easy! Strap it on to the outside of the plane. It's quite a sight to see a shiny new aluminum boat strapped securely to the plane's float and with a roar of the engine and enough speed attained, plane and boat lift off the water's surface as one.

Experiencing a flight on a float plane is exhilarating, and something we were fortunate to enjoy at least twice a year. Let me try to describe it for you. No matter the size of the plane, whether Cessna 185, Beaver, Single Otter, or Twin Otter, the feelings of excitement are the same.

Once seated beside the pilot and buckled in, the engine starts and you putt-putt your way out from the dock. Even at an idle, the engine and propeller have enough thrust to take the plane on a leisurely cruise to an area that will allow a long unimpeded takeoff.

As the engine warms up, the pilot goes through a check-out routine, and when satisfied, looks over at you and asks "Are you ready?" Your smile and thumbs up is your reply. Here we go!

He makes an adjustment to the throttle, and very quickly the engine is screaming at a high pitch. At first the plane is slow to respond, but with increasing speed, it quickly skims along the water and gets *on step*, the speed where plane and water are connected, but you are hydroplaning. Any reference points viewed from the side window blur and disappear under the increasing speed, and with a glance down, you notice a swath of spray being thrown from the float on your side. There's a surge as the floats break free of the lake surface.

While gaining altitude, the pilot follows the lake contour and makes some adjustments. Staying handy to water is safest should the pilot need to make a quick landing, but eventually a change of course takes place, and you are flying over land with a bird's eye view of the surrounding countryside.

During spring, we chartered a float plane so we could return to civilization to do our shopping, pick up our mail, and take care of any appointments. In late September or early October, we charted the plane for our second annual trip. There was always an air of excitement in autumn as we prepared for winter's isolation. Although we were secluded year round, starting in the fall, birds were heading to warmer climates, animals were starting to hunker down, and a peaceful quiet descended over the land.

It was always good to get the trip over with and get back home! We would off-load the winter's supplies from the plane, stand on the dock and watch the plane take off. Once it was a mere speck in the distance, well beyond hearing, we were left with nothing but a deafening silence.

It was at that moment we became acutely aware our last physical link with humanity just flew away, and we had the sense we were fully immersed in the wilderness, with no one but ourselves left on the planet. Exciting!

∞

Winter came early in the north, and many times we flew home to find a dusting of snow on the ground. The last vegetables from the garden—potatoes, carrots, and cabbage—were dug up and stored for the long winter ahead.

There is such a contrast between open water and ice-covered lakes. A frozen lake is static and seems lifeless, while open water, with its accompanying waves, is so dynamic. We liked both states, but felt more alive and vibrant in summer, when the lake was teeming with activity and wildlife. But winter had its good points as well.

As I looked across our snow-covered lake on a cold winter's day, the wind whipping the snow into sheets that drifted into swirled random patterns as it blew across the surface, the scene gave me the sense I was in the middle of a frozen tundra devoid of all life other than the two of us.

Yet, a walk across the frozen white tundra on a more hospitable day, clearly showed the tracks of animal activity. The glide imprints of an otter, the hurried prints of a hare sprinting for cover, the jumbled hoof tracks of a moose foraging along the shoreline, or the large paw prints of a wolf traveling through its territory, were evidence we were not alone. There was life in the animal kingdom, albeit at a slower pace in this harsh environment.

Below the frozen lake surface, the fish slowed down in their much-darkened world, dark not only from less sunlight due to a shorter day length, but from the snow that covered the ice surface. The thick layer of ice sealed off the vagaries of weather, creating a tranquil place, until the ice relinquished its grip. A definite quiet descended on the area when the lake was frozen.

The two facets of lake living I miss greatly are the winter freeze-up and the spring thaw. Both are compelling times, and I'll try to describe what occurs during these transitions. These were the two times of the year when we were really on our own. The float planes are out of the water during freeze-up, and off the ice during spring thaw. We couldn't be reached by bush plane until the lake either froze, so a plane on skis could land, or there was enough open water for a plane on floats. A helicopter, out of reach due to the expense, was the only other alternative.

Freeze-up was never the same from one year to the next. Usually it was well under way by mid-November, but there was one cold autumn when the lake was completely skimmed over by the end of October. Depending on temperatures and wind, freeze-up could occur all at once on a frigid calm night, or sections of the lake could freeze over the course of a few days.

During those times, ice fog could develop from plummeting air temperatures, while the water was still warm. Drifting off the lake, the ice fog created a coating of hoar frost on all surfaces, and trees had a thick, crystalline layer of frost. A glance outside made it appear there had been snow overnight, but it was just everything covered in a thick rime. The immediate shoreline, in contact with the fog, got the brunt of this icy coating.

Branches of Jack pine have needles that surround a central stem, much like a long bristle-bottle brush. Hoar frost coated the slender needles, adding up to an inch of delicate, white, crystalline encrustation. When the angle of the sun was just right, the sunlight refracted through the frosty coating, transforming the stark, cold landscape into a glittering winter wonderland. It was really quite beautiful.

Freezing lakes are noisy. Amazingly, freezing water produces a variety of sounds, the volume of which is astounding. Most noise occurred at night, as temperatures dropped, with the first two to four weeks of freeze-up being the most active.

We lived inside a super insulated home, but we could still hear the lake groaning loudly. Sometimes it rumbled like nearby thunder. Other times it boomed like an explosion, with reverberations echoing off the hillsides. When the lake ice or frozen ground made a sudden expansive move, the power was enormous. Although not common, when that happened, our house shuddered and shook as the tremor went through.

Once the lake skimmed over, it was generally another four to six weeks before there was enough ice to land a bush plane. The ice formed quickly, providing the weather cooperated. Significant snowfall right after the lake skimmed over could be detrimental since the snow acted as an insulating layer. In that event, the ice would take longer to form. Compounding the situation, if there was enough snow on top of the ice, the weight of the snow forced water up in some areas, creating slush on the ice surface.

From the air, "spider holes" were easily seen, usually in bays, but found anywhere on the lake. Having a central hole with irregular fingers radiating outward, they looked like a wet area surrounded by snow. The fingers served as drainage channels through which water on the surface drained back into the hole. Perhaps they were created when warmer lake water was pushed upward through a crack in the ice and flooded the lake surface. The initial flaw in the ice could be a small crack, an animal access point likely used by an otter, or even trapped air bubbles that weakened the ice in that spot. Regardless, the spider holes are dangerous and should be avoided.

ᏟᏆ

Spring breakup was a wonderful experience too. Not only were the days getting longer but animals were more active and we were secure in the knowledge we had survived another winter—not to mention it was fantastic to be outdoors on warm days. But, lying north of 56 degrees latitude, spring had the nasty habit of giving us false hope one day, with 50°F temperatures and melting and then the next day dashing that hope with snow and a temperature of 10°F! Once over that hurdle, breakup granted one of the most remarkable events.

Breakup began with snow pack diminishing until all the snow had melted off the ice. Then the ice started to melt along the shoreline, slowly at first—but as more water was exposed and warmed, the ice receded more quickly. Every night the narrow band of open water along the shorelines refroze, but each day a little more headway was made as the area thawed and became more expansive. With the aid of the shining sun, melt water formed, which collected on top of the ice, forming large shallow pools. Water streamed into holes that started as small cracks. The force of the draining water created small eddies that swirled in the holes. Under the setting sun and cooler night temperatures, the melting was arrested, and the shallow pools drained. If the melted surface refroze overnight, a white blanket greeted us the next morning, and as melting occurred that day, the surface would eventually turn gray. Sooner or later, the night temperature stayed above freezing, allowing the rate of ice melt to accelerate.

Lake ice doesn't melt like a big ice cube. As it melts, the ice honeycombs and melt water trickles down through small, nearly invisible fractures. It is through these cracks and small air bubbles, which were frozen in time during freeze-up, that melt water flows, eroding the ice as it permeates the layer. The lake goes through stages of melt, with the color of the ice changing from white to gray, to dark gray, to finally black, as the thickness of the ice decreases.

When the ice turned dark, we knew we were getting close to ice out. By the time the remaining ice was 6 inches thick, we could pick up chunks that shattered into dozens of smaller fragments, resembling sheets of glass that had been dropped.

Wind played a big role in how fast the ice melted. Think of it as a big fan blowing air across the surface of the ice. Once the ice sheet had melted along all the shoreline, it became a free-floating mass, able to be pushed around by the wind. Holes further out would start to open as wind kept working their edges. If the edges were weak enough, a tinkling sound was heard as the wave and wind action loosened small shards of ice. Bays shed their icy shackles the first, the water no longer confined by a frozen layer. Soon thereafter, smaller ice sheets broke away from the main body and were driven by the wind currents on to land or into each other. More and more chunks broke off, and soon there were wide open expanses of water, not only along the shoreline but further out.

The direction the ice sheets moved, was of course, determined by the wind. It was both fascinating and scary to see a sheet of ice maybe three-quarters of a mile long being pushed down the lake, toward our shoreline. Once the sheet has momentum, it's hard to stop, and the advancing ice keeps piling up on shore. All the while, it is fracturing and breaking up, and there was no mistaking the sound, a sound resembling high-volume static from a radio. If we were outside, we would hear the crunching and grinding of ice being thrust up onto the shore. We had several rocky points of land that jutted into the lake where we could go for a first-hand, closeup look at ice piling up on the rocks.

It was alarming when the sheet of ice was heading for our dock. The dock was no match and lost every battle against the ice. It would push the dock up onto shore or tear it apart. We've seen it happen. When we heard lumber snapping into pieces, we knew the dock was not faring too well.

Once the ice is on the move, within a day, the lake could be ice-free. Between the melting power of the sun, the fanning action of the wind across the ice surface, the action of waves on the ice sheet edges, and the sheet being physically driven onshore, the mile-long expanse of ice disappeared astonishingly quickly.

Here today, gone tomorrow. That fast! We went from hopelessness that the ice would never go, to let's go canoeing—all in one day.

During the last tenacious remnants of winter, scattered piles of ice on various shorelines disappeared quickly and, with luck, would be the last frozen white stuff until fall. May 13th was our target for ice out. Anything before that date was a bonus. One year we were ice-free as early as April 29th and, on the flip side, we endured an excruciatingly slow melt that lasted until the last day in May.

$$\infty$$

Open water, confirmation the long winter was over, was my overall favorite time of the year. It was pure joy to go down to the water's edge throughout the day. Many a morning, as soon as I awoke, I'd walk down the hill to the lake shore to watch and observe. Dead calm, the lake surface mirror like, I could always spot pairs of ducks and loons. Sometimes, with a splash and a frenzied beating of wings, an odd duck jostled for position among an established pair. The argument would be settled for a time, and then the contest would resume.

We built a sturdy dock to serve as a tie up point for visiting float planes and our boat. It created a wonderful observation platform throughout the year. If you stood with me on the dock, we might see the splash of jumping fish or, over by the rocky protrusion of the nearby point, the surface become pockmarked with small concentric rings, signifying bait fish feeding on floating specks of food. When the light was just right, we might see bugs of all kinds skittering across the surface, leaving more visible tracks than the eye could focus on.

Therein lies the secret of observation: don't focus, but let your eyes take it all in. Allow your peripheral vision to capture a world full of animation. By not zeroing in on a specific image, you will see more of the subtle movements. A gaze into the water may reveal a school of bait fish passing through or a myriad of submerged insects, some crawling around on the bottom, which will soon become predators.

Dragonflies, hundreds of them, will emerge from their underwater world to patrol the air, thereby helping to control the bug population. How wonderful it was to have a large dragonfly land on my arm, a moose fly in its jaws, and hear the chomping sounds as it devoured its meal. That meant one less blood-sucking, flying insect to torment man and beast. Rest in the sunshine for a minute digesting your meal dragonfly and then go forth and catch another bug!

On a warm day, with the sun shining high overhead, we sometimes saw the 20-inch pike that rested in the shade of our dock. It used to speed off with a quick flick of its tail whenever we would walk on to the dock, but it soon became accustomed to us and hung suspended in the shallow water, close enough to touch.

In the blink of an eye, the stillness could be overtaken by a wind, waves driven on to the beach in rapid, frothing succession. We had better hold on to our hats if we were to go down to the beach when high winds were coming from the southwest. That direction allowed the wind to come straight up the lake, roiling it, violently bobbing our boat at its berth, the vessel secured only by two small diameter ropes. Thanks to the wind, there wouldn't be much in the way of biting insects, and the boat would remain where it was, steadfastly tethered to the dock, bouncing as every wave hit the bow. No boat ride that day.

When parked on my boat chair, drifting on a calm, warm night, I reflected on how privileged I was to live on a wilderness lake. Unspoiled, pollution-free, with no other human for miles and miles, and surrounded by millions of acres of forest, there was no better setting than my little aluminum boat to take in the whole experience.

I might throw a hook overboard to see if I could entice a fish but I'd long since been fished out. I'm not big on eating fish so any fishing I did was catch and release. Once my line was out I'd sit quietly in my comfy boat seat observing the shoreline for signs of animal activity. The shoreline was a great place to observe wildlife. If I was lucky, I might see a mother loon sneak out of her nest or later in the season, see a couple of fluffy hatchlings snagging a ride on their mother's back. Maybe I'd see a mother duck with baby *quack quacks* following along in single file. I've seen the occasional moose and bear swimming in the lake. Both are quite adept at long distance swims in comparison to me who would briefly explore the lake bottom before expiring!

Hop in the boat's bow seat and take a ride with me down to a narrow section we needed to pass through in order to access the lower part of our lake. On shore, notice the cacophony of singing birds, flitting from tree to tree or the graceful glide of an eagle or osprey circling high overhead. In this lower section there used to be an eagle's aerie. A precariously leaning tree, old and dead from the ravages of fire, yet strong enough to support the mass of twisted sticks and debris that composed the nest, was the foundation upon which the nest was built. Every other year the site became home to a mating pair of mature eagles and their two eaglets. When the tree ultimately succumbed to wind and decay, the eagles built a new nest on a nearby island.

One summer we motored down to check on the eaglets already fledged and resting in the nest. As we pulled up in the boat, one of them jumped from the nest, made a bee line for us, then slowly glided low overhead in a circle. When it returned to its tree top perch, it peered at us as if to say, "Look at me. I can fly."

It wouldn't be long before they would be gone for the winter. "Have a safe flight my friend. We'll see you when you return."

If I was feeling spiffy after dinner, I'd motor down the lake a ways and row back home. There's something special about rowing a small boat or paddling a canoe; the way the oars or paddles caught the water and propelled the craft forward under my own steam.

There was no rush to row back home. So many times, I stopped in the middle of the lake and lay across the bottom of the boat to drift while gazing at the sky. It's amazing what comes into view when we stop and study. I stopped for long enough to observe wisps of clouds either grow or dissipate. How fascinating to watch small clouds dissolve into nothing.

Or watch as the reverse happened. Small clouds changing shape and growing larger. All it took was focus without distraction. Many a time I watched as clouds, colored white to black and every hue in between, moved quickly across the sky while at other times, they lingered seemingly in place.

Once, a thunderstorm boiled up overhead. Clouds built before my eyes. Interesting until lightning bolts started flying. My aluminum boat became a perilous place to be. Please, little motor, pick up the pace and get me home!

Sunsets from a favorite land vista are nice, but seeing one from the perspective of a watercraft is special. The scenery constantly changes, and the reflection of the water adds vivid colors. Many a night, I wouldn't come back home until the sun had set. The perfect ending to a day was to be in the right spot on the lake to watch the sun drop down on the saddle between two nearby hills, the hills seemingly parting to allow the sun to bed for the night.

Alas all good things come to an end. Before I knew it, there was a chill in the air. Summer came and went much too quickly. It seemed like yesterday that I had put the boat back in the water from its winter berth.

Come fall, as the leaves dropped from the trees and a cold wind blew from the north, the year's crop of hatchlings had already left. The remaining loons were visible but silent, floating on the waves, reluctant to leave the place they had called home for the last five months. Their excited spring cackle replaced with a quiet resignation that a long flight south was imminent. The last straggler could often be seen from the dock in our bay, even as a biting wind howled, and the season's first snow coated the ground. Who could blame them for not wanting to leave?

I have so many memories of our many years at Hockley Lake. It was a source of refuge and safety when firestorms rolled through the area and burned massive amounts of forestland. And it spared my life when I had to swim after my boat shortly after ice out one year. But those can be stories for another day.

Thank you Hockley Lake, Saskatchewan, a source of pride and a treasured experience in my life.

TEMPERATE UPLAND RIVERS

Temperate Upland River ecoregions are dominated and defined by mid-latitude non-floodplain rivers, including headwater drainages and tributaries of large river systems. These rivers are characterized by moderate gradients and the absence of a cyclically flooded, fringing floodplain.

GROWING UP WITH RIVERS

Tim Palmer

Home lay on a broad ridge where the river began. You couldn't see the flashing bends, the rippling pools, the waterfalls, the rapids. In fact, you couldn't even see water at all unless you looked carefully.

Our land was the uppermost ground. It didn't look much different from millions of other rural homesites across the United States. But when raindrops and snowflakes fell on our family soil, they began their journey downhill, bound inevitably for the Gulf of Mexico, fifteen hundred miles away, by river.

Knowing how I feel about rivers today, I might easily imagine myself being born on the banks of some powerful freshwater artery or at least along a tributary large enough for catching a fish. But maybe that humble beginning—high in the watershed, stitched into the fabric of Appalachian Mountain foothills—maybe that is what made me who I am. I do know that this story began there.

Kids never think about where the water in the driveway puddles comes from, and where it goes, and I didn't either. But gradually I pieced together the logic that the puddles and the low swale alongside the garden were somehow connected to the spring, which lay downhill from them, at the other end of a field.

The spring was The Source—one of the first sources of anything that I knew and identified as such in my life. When I picture this scene from many years ago, or think about drawing a schematic of our property, I now envision the spring as a brilliantly fluid core at the center, colored in deep reflective blue while even the house sits at the periphery in subdued gray. Because of wet ground in the lowlands where the spring appeared, a lot of shrubs and high weeds surrounded it. But a path led to the water, and even at a very young age I followed every path I could find.

My great uncle, who lived just up the hill with my beloved grandfather, had shored-up the walls of the spring with blocks of sandstone, giving the water more depth than it otherwise would have had. We didn't drink this water, but during the dry weeks of late summer, when our well couldn't stand the strain of extra pumping, my grandfather and I dipped buckets of water from the spring and carried them to our gardens. Walking down the cultivated rows, we poured the water into bowls molded by dirt we had carefully pushed up around tomato plants and cantaloupe vines. Without being told, I knew that the springwater was a life-force of great importance.

It seemed not only important, but almost magical. No matter how much water we took out—keep in mind we were just an old man and a young boy hefting buckets by hand—the spring never dried up.

In the winter I learned that it never froze, even though all the other surface water did and even though the ground near the spring turned rock-hard. After the snow melted, the spring flowed stronger, pouring liberally over its outlet. The water ran down through a field to a deepening woods. Then it disappeared into the unknown.

Where did it go?

As I grew older, I could count my years by how far downstream I had explored. Our creek soon penetrated a forest of oak and hickory, darkened here and there by an eastern hemlock growing in the shade of steep hillsides that the stream had shaped like a sculptor molding an outsized pile of clay, in this case, the entire Appalachian Plateau.

Every bend opened new wonders to me. I spotted woodpeckers drumming on dead elms. I sneaked up on an agitated flock of crows until they scattered, leaving a great horned owl sternly staring down at me from a hollowed-out sycamore high above the creek. At the widest ponded place in my stream I flushed a duck. Being an upland boy, I had never seen waterfowl of any kind. It was only a mallard—the kind of duck that city kids tossed bread crumbs to all the time. But thrilled at the iridescent green of its head, I ran home with the news. "Mom, you won't believe what I saw!"

During my high school years, these Saturday-morning outings expanded to day-long expeditions. I packed lunch and hiked downstream as far as I could, my increasing endurance now a match for my curiosity. My stream grew in volume and the riffles gained some force while the flow dropped off sandstone ledges and then filtered into wetlands and later trickled out. The water pooled up in places big enough for me to jump in. The stream and its valley were amazingly wild for being only forty miles from Pittsburgh.

Then one day I heard the incongruous rumble of truck noise ahead of me. Approaching cautiously, almost afraid of what I would find, I saw that my wild stream tunneled into the darkness of a culvert beneath a trash-littered, four-lane highway. Then, with all its distance covered, with its own life of intimacy past, my little stream entered the Ohio River.

At that time the Ohio was the largest barge-floating cesspool in America. In a few short feet my family waters mixed and then disappeared into the rainbow swirled, oily flow of that eastern behemoth, once the biologically richest river in America but for generations dedicated to industrial barging.

In one culminating instant I understood what a stream should be and what it shouldn't. I sensed something tragic in what happens to the unfortunate raindrops and headwater rivulets that flow into the wrong river. This awareness came solely from what I *saw*–simply the way it *looked* to me. I wanted to capture it all in a picture, but couldn't. I didn't even own a camera.

Huge, the Ohio stretched a quarter mile across, its abuses embedded in the aging steel mills rusting along its edge, in the traffic pounding its banks, and in railroad tracks that cordoned off the water. Furthermore, it stunk. What had once been the ultimate life force had become a conduit for waste in volumes and concentrations that defined the term "public health hazard."

The combined effect assaulted my senses completely, but something else troubled me even more. Dirty water, after all, could be cleaned up. The highway and railroad tracks, after all, had to go someplace. Something else, I knew, was even more amiss with the Ohio River.

Then I realized: it had no flow. It didn't *move*. Later I would learn that the Ohio is dammed back-to-back twenty-six times in 981 miles, scarcely a hundred yards of free-flowing river to be found in its entire length.

The Ohio showed me what could happen to streams when they became rivers. At the time, I took my stream's dammed and polluted outcome simply as a lesson in the way the world is. An accompanying sense of fatalism took years to shed. What I saw, of course, doesn't happen to every stream, and even where it does, there's no reason it must stay that way forever. But these realizations would come later. Before I could imagine better possibilities, I had to live more, see more, and learn more about other streams.

∞

During those same years, another river flowed into my life and affected me even more deeply. The Youghiogheny (yock-a-GEN-ee) cut through the mountain town of Ohiopyle, Pennsylvania. This sleepy, two-block burg in Appalachia clung with a time-tested grip to a hillside above the banks of the river. Ancestors of mine had settled there nearly three hundred years earlier. Some hearty relatives remained, and once each summer my family journeyed back to visit my great aunt and uncle and to stay for awhile at a white frame house, owned by my grandmother.

A formidable set of creaking steps led up to a full-length porch where a two-person wicker swing hung by chains from the rafters. This comfortable slice of Americana lay deeply shaded under the leggy limbs of sugar maples. Most important, the porch looked down to the river.

Right there in town, just a couple of stone-throws below the house, the Youghiogheny plunged over one of the largest waterfalls in the East. Then it ripped into rock-ribbed rapids and curled around bends overhung by sandstone crags and the silhouettes of gnarly hemlocks that had been pruned and scarred by storms and by the picturesque rot that inevitably comes with time.

As a boy, I gloried in Ohiopyle because it was so easy to make believe that I lived in another era. I could imagine the Iroquois of James Fenimore Cooper stories appearing on the jagged outcrops of sandstone, and meeting them, and joining them.

More important, the Youghiogheny flowed big enough that I could imagine traveling on it. In this consummate adventure, I would launch a log raft in the big eddy below the falls. After kicking-off from shore, I would brave the rapids, one by one. I wanted to do this so badly that I had to be careful not to think too much about it. But the fantasy returned again and again: I would kiss security and boyhood good-by and face the great unknown as the river swept me mercilessly away from all that I had known in order to learn what I needed to know.

Where did the river go? I wondered.

What would I see if I went there?

Then one day I spotted three older boys blowing up a yellow raft and carrying it into the river. They cinched their army surplus life jackets and paddled without hesitation into the non-negotiable suck of the current.

They were living out my dream. As I did when I saw my first duck, I ran back to my grandmother's house with the news. Envious of what those older kids were doing, I knew that to navigate the Youghiogheny still lay beyond me. But I couldn't help wondering if someday, I could take the plunge downriver myself.

On a quieter hike a few years later—all alone, as usual—I climbed over big stacks of Youghiogheny rocks and emerged on a flat ledge above a whitewashed rapid. I sat down to rest, and to look, and to listen.

Warm, moist evening air scented with July's rhododendron flowers filled my head, but nothing was on my mind, absolutely nothing. I just leaned against a timeless rocky backrest and watched the water flow. The sun set toward the steamy profile of Appalachian forest, and the last yellow rays of light glinted through the branches and made sparkles on the water, which after awhile began to play tricks on my eyes. Spray shot off like fireworks, and the constant movement now and then seemed to stop while the rest of my world launched into dizzying upstream motion.

I was entranced.

The sound filled me up as well, and the rest of the world could have been a thousand miles away.

Then, suddenly, it occurred to me: "This place is perfect."

All this happened after I had followed my own home stream the whole way to the Ohio River, and so I knew why this place on the Youghiogheny was perfect. Quite simply, it had been left alone. It was natural. Like my Ohio River revelation, this one derived solely from what I saw. I hardly knew anything about rivers.

When it got dark I had to go home, and this time I couldn't tell anybody what I had seen or what had happened, because nothing had really happened at all. Yet somehow my world had changed. Now I knew something that I hadn't known before.

I didn't realize that this had been a defining moment for me, and I was certainly not aware that it marked a step toward a lifetime of knowing rivers. But there beside the Youghiogheny, on a warm summer night, I had somehow bonded with the flow of water. I loved it. And I wanted more.

But the time for rivers had not yet come in my life. With adventurous dreams shelved way back where it wasn't evident if I'd ever live them out, I left for college. Eventually I found my way to the field of landscape architecture. I embraced the basic premise of that fine profession: both art and the beauty of nature can be integrated while designing outdoor spaces for practical use. However, I was troubled by the mandate that put development first. This, I soon realized, owed to who paid the landscape architects for their services.

Our professors at Penn State assigned realistic projects: say, arrange fifty condominiums on five acres being split from a local farm at the edge of town. I enjoyed the game of shuffling blocks on models and shaping contours, of curving entrance roads and planting borders so they looked like the real woods where I had grown up. But I always wondered, were condominiums the best use of that property? Siting fifty of them while incorporating usable and attractive open space was a worthwhile challenge, but I still had to ask, should anything be built there at all? The land might better be left as a farm. Following this line of thought, it seemed to me that riverfronts might better be left to the forces of floods, the work of beavers, and the rule of natural law.

Near the end of my junior year an opportunity to confront these kinds of questions came my way. I had drawn up a plan for a bicycle trail in the town that surrounded Penn State University. I designed a type of plan that would later be called a "greenway." After I showed my drawings to a group of local residents, a tall, gray haired man approached me and asked if I'd be interested in working on a watershed-based plan for a large stream called Pine Creek.

"What's a watershed?" I asked.

He patiently answered that it was all the land that drains into a particular stream. I immediately thought of my home ground, where I had grown up at the top of the ridge, which drained toward the spring, and then into the stream, and later into the Ohio River. A forester by profession, Dr. Peter Fletcher wanted me to see what a nature-based planning approach might suggest for how the Pine Creek watershed of northern Pennsylvania could best be used and protected.

I jumped at the opportunity. The first task was to canoe the river and inventory everything I saw.

Through a whole year of mapping the floodplains and the wetlands, of plotting the steep slopes and the wildlands, of checking in the field for the most beautiful views, the essential wildlife habitat, and the nuggets of local character such as giant trees or big rock outcrops, I fell deeply in love with that elegant river on the eastern incline of the Appalachian Mountains. I went there often, fall, winter, and spring. I never wanted to leave. It was the place of my dreams.

Learning about rivers and how they work, I realized that my early childhood impressions had hit the mark, two bulls' eyes. The Ohio River was ugly because it had been damaged, poisoned, ruined. The Youghiogheny was beautiful because it was intact, its natural cycles still functioning.

As a designer and then a planner, I learned that the most important thing in caring for a river was to protect the land that floods. Cleaning up the pollution from towns and thousands of septic tanks was also necessary, and proper stewardship was needed for the headwaters where the runoff began. I learned that the quantity as well as the quality of water in the river spelled success or failure to all the life around it. I learned that riverlife included everything from algae to sycamores, everything from mayflies that were snatched up by rainbow trout to beavers that checked erosion on tributary streams. All the pieces had to be handled carefully or the whole wouldn't add up to a healthy system.

Armed with new knowledge and a lot of enthusiasm but clueless about the scope of political difficulties lurking ahead in my path, I wanted my work to make a difference. So, after graduation, rather than taking a job designing real condo complexes on farms at the edges of towns, I decided to put my Pine Creek plans to work.

A fishermen's group called Trout Unlimited pitched in money to get me started, and I dove headfirst into the whirlpool of politics that surrounds every question about the future of every river in America. I persuaded the State Bureau of Forestry to set aside a few of the finest tributary streams as Wild or Natural Areas–the highest form of watershed protection. I tried to get local governments to zone their floodplains to prevent development that would otherwise eliminate the best habitat and cost millions of dollars in damage when the flood inevitably came. A few years later, after the greatest deluge in history scoured the valley, the floodplain zoning approach succeeded. I also persuaded The Nature Conservancy and the state to buy some of the most important stream frontage for open space. And every day I paddled a canoe.

I canoed every day because I lived in a cabin on the other side of the creek from the road. At first I borrowed a boat from a friend. Later I bought my own. I paddled across Pine Creek to the village of Cammal to pick up my mail, to buy groceries, and to drive out to anywhere I had to go.

Whenever I got the chance, I slipped the canoe into the water for a longer trip. Enduring my share of mistakes, I eventually learned how to read the rapids. I learned when to go ahead, when to stop and look, and when to carry the canoe around. I learned how to angle into big waves and how to push through holes that could otherwise completely swamp the boat.

My Pine Creek work led to a job with the local county as a land-use planner, a career that lasted eight years and required that I consider all aspects of rivers and their uses. I worked with streams as small as Trout Run, where I dipped a bucket to get drinking water just outside my cabin, and as wide as the Susquehanna—the largest river on the East Coast of the United States.

To truly know that great waterway, which ran down the centerline of our county, I decided to spend my vacation canoeing from the uppermost point where I could float my boat all the way to the Chesapeake Bay. For eight days and 230 miles, with my friend Bob Banks, I thrilled at the vastness of a long river and at the epic nature of its journey, mountains to sea. Every bend brought another view—another perspective on the world. Camping on islands, I felt as wild and adventurous as Huckleberry Finn.

Each day was different from any that I had ever lived, yet each was also the same in its free-flowing routine of breaking camp, dipping our paddles into glassy pools or agitated riffles, swimming alongside the boat in the heat of the afternoon, and sleeping under a dome of sycamores. I entered the realm of rivertime, when life moves with the cycles of season and sun, wind and current. Morning mist burns off as the day warms; the wind blusters as the heat on the land intensifies; the speed of the current ebbs and accelerates in a sequence of pool, riffle, pool, riffle.

As I lived out these moments, hours, and days with intense awareness of my environment, the Susquehanna took a stronger and stronger hold on me. I realized that, along a river, I could search endlessly for beauty—and find it—a practice that increasingly motivated me. I started taking pictures and became fascinated with the challenge of capturing the kaleidoscope of scenes and the ever-changing moods of flowing water.

I learned a lot on that trip. Floating along for miles and miles, I gained a greater understanding of the wholeness of a river. The many parts that I had seen separately and that appeared with their own placenames on the map all began to link together as one. With this awareness of connections, I better grasped the value of the entire river. Instead of separate parts, which can easily be split off and then commodified, I saw the river altogether, each part critical to the rest, the whole stream like one big organism, elegant and complex. Knowing the river in this way, I could better understand the damage of a strip mine here, a feedlot there, a clearcut here, a highway encroachment there.

In all this I sensed the close ties between forest and fish, between mountaintop and sandbar, between flood flows and groundwater surfacing far from the Susquehanna itself. It all seemed evident, but I wanted to know more about all these things and to be able to show the connections and the beauty of the river's wholeness to other people.

Out there overnight, one thing I knew for sure was that rivers offered the best way to travel. Everything I saw and did—watching a mink scrambling along the shore, cooking over a fire, dodging rocks in rapids—all of it was just fine, but the river as a means of going somewhere was the main thing. The Susquehanna had become my way of seeing America.

Deeply satisfied after that trip, yet highly motivated as well, I wanted to see the other great rivers of the East. Even more, I wanted to see the streams that flowed off the steep slopes of the Rocky Mountains, the Cascades of the Pacific Northwest, and most of all, the magnificent granite rise of the Sierra Nevada in California.

Then, through a friend I had met at a river planning conference, I heard about the Stanislaus in the foothills of the Sierra Nevada. This river splashed down from snowy mountains, into a green belt of cedar and Sequoia trees, and then past rugged foothills. It churned through the deepest limestone canyon on the Pacific Coast where more people went whitewater rafting than anywhere else in the West. This canyon was also the most contested dam-site in American history. In 1979 the river remained a paradise, but it was soon to be lost, forever, and for no good reason other than the lingering momentum to dam every wild river in a state whose official animal was the grizzly bear—long extinct.

I quit my planning job to write a book about a band of Stanislaus activists who called themselves Friends of the River. With them I floated the rapids, camped on sunny beaches, swam in lucid pools at twilight, and labored day and night writing about our river, weighing arguments for its use and protection, and persuading people from local officials up to the Governor and President to try to spare one of the most extraordinary places I had ever known, and ever will know.

We lost that fight. The flatwater of New Melones Reservoir entombed the Stanislaus River canyon and all the sandy beaches, the bubbling rapids, the riverfront caves, and the village sites that Miwok Indians had occupied for millennia. Each scene of artistic splendor disappeared, inch by agonizing inch, foot by excruciating foot, until it was gone, utterly gone under a muddy gloam six hundred feet deep. For me and for thousands of other people who had come to know and love the place, the death of the Stanislaus brought a wave of despair, but more important, it triggered a resolve that nothing so precious should ever be lost again.

With this great river gone, and a great emptiness where the Stanislaus had lived so briefly but vitally in my heart, I returned to write a book about my own river, the Youghiogheny, which survived as I had known it. The river had actually improved with the treatment of coal-mine drainage that earlier stained many tributaries orange with iron and acid.

While I had been away, the secluded Appalachian enclave of my youth had become the most popular whitewater run in America. The family homestead had been sold for a state park in Ohiopyle, so I could no longer use my grandmother's house. But wanting no encumbrances, I lived happily out of my van and worked on my book above the banks of that long-familiar stream.

I reasoned that to tell the story of a river, I had to start at the beginning. Therefore my first task was to seek out the headwaters, high on the Youghiogheny-Potomac divide. No path led to this special place. But beyond a thicket of rhododendron and greenbrier I found a diminutive trace of water that flowed just like the spring of my childhood, though this spring was fully wild, untended by anyone's great uncle. From this new Source in my life, I followed the tumbling route downstream. Ironically, like the first stream of my youth, Youghiogheny waters ended up taking me the whole way to the Ohio River.

After living for months by the Youghiogheny, I finally set my canoe alongside the pool below the Ohiopyle Falls. I drew in a deep breath as I cinched my own life jacket. Then I kicked-off from shore the way I had dreamed of doing so many years before.

The rapids of the Youghiogheny were larger, rockier, and whiter than anything I had ever run, but I had learned the finer points of leaning the bottom of the boat away from the jets of crosscurrent, of catching eddies and stopping in the middle of swift flows, of surfing on the slick green waves. Doing all this on the river of my youth now exhilarated me, and the airy lightness of bubbles beneath the boat lightened my spirit as well. I couldn't help laughing out loud at my good fortune—being in a boat, on a river—a natural river. Nothing could be finer.

I learned to identify real danger compared to the usual whitewater rush. I learned to use the flow of the river rather than to fight it. Except, sometimes I had to fight as well: the Youghiogheny pounded into the face of an ominous boulder. I had to move to the left. I *had* to! Paddle harder! *Harder!*

I learned about total engagement—being so focused on the complexities of the river ahead that the rest of the world completely disappears. Then, when I returned, the rest of the world looked fresher and brighter.

In seeing the whole river, from beginning to end, I found that it offered values that are practical, ecological, social, and economic. Furthermore, it served up important lessons, along with metaphors of many kinds. One of these has survived the ages because it fits so well: the source and headwaters symbolize youth. The small but increasing flow offers promises of many kinds. Growing larger, the river reflects adolescence, and the rapids are chaotic, risky, exciting. Then the widening waters signify maturity. Some rapids here are huge, and in other places headwinds blow upriver through miles of flatwater. Finally, with a broad and gentle current, the lower river denotes old age, the mysterious and infinite ocean ahead. For anyone floating on those waters, the approach to the sea is inevitable, unstoppable with the force of the whole river pushing from behind.

Like the rest of life, rivers flow unceasingly—forever different yet forever the same. They bring life to the land around them, and at the same time they reflect everything that we do to the land that lies upstream. Traveling on rivers, I always had to accommodate changes, surprises, new impressions, greater meanings. Rivers are lifelines in so many ways.

These early experiences on waterways led me to an unending pursuit of knowing, writing about, and photographing rivers. When I later lived along the

Salmon River of Idaho, and rafted its four hundred mile length, I learned about the wild Chinook and sockeye salmon that gave the river its name. I realized that these charismatic fish were endangered and would likely go extinct unless changes were made to the dams blocking their path downstream in the lower Snake River. For me, the salmon came to symbolize the importance of all life connected to the rivers—a community of creatures unmatched, irreplaceable, essential.

Later, in the southern Sierra, I worked with a group of fishermen to defeat a plan to dam the Kings River, which flows through the deepest canyon in America. There and along other streams, the momentum of destruction that had tragically sealed the fate of the Stanislaus was stopped. But what happens now in the twenty-first century—in a new era of runaway population growth and the abandonment of political responsibilities—remains to be seen.

I never returned to Sixmile Run—the stream that our family springwater joined on its way to the Ohio River. But I've been back to the Youghiogheny many times where that showcase of whitewater was included in a state park, and protected. I still go down and sit on the rocks whenever I can, and when I relax with a timeless sandstone boulder as a backrest on a warm and sultry summer evening—especially when rhododendron flowers scent the air—the power of it all is so strong that the years evaporate and disappear, leaving me right where I was the very first time. I'm back there again, seeing a wondrous river as a new and vital force in my life.

Since I first sat there, bonding to the flow of water, I've canoed or rafted on nearly 400 different rivers. I've written books, worked for groups to save their rivers, and spent months at a time along dozens of different streams. Living out my lotic dreams, I've learned all I could about everything that rivers touch.

Hundreds of rivers in every part of the country have drawn me to their edges and their centers, to sunrises, sunsets, and moonlit nights along watery green shores from one ocean to another. And it all began at that spring, beyond the edge of our backyard in the Appalachian foothills.

SEVEN RIVERS

Rob Carney

People who know me know this: I don't pretend to be an expert on the legal codes of New Zealand. But back in March something happened there that keeps on running through my mind. Their House of Representatives, which must be a whole bunch different than ours, passed a bill giving human rights to the Whanganui River. How's that for treatment of a natural resource? Pretty good. And what I keep thinking—now that a river can claim personhood and dignity—is, What do I want to suggest for human rights next?

Probably stars. They deserve to be noticed. Once a month we'll have darkness by decree. Each year, we'll have twelve new ways to look up, a dozen needed oases.

And Puget Sound, of course. Whether seen from a ferry or not. Whether or not it's sundown on Seattle's million windows so the skyline is mirroring gold-orange, rose, and red, and the Olympic Mountains are both in front of you and behind you, and seagulls ride rivers of updraft, and this time and place and wind should be vested with rights.

The trees near Crescent City too—they're older than Christianity. I'll call each sequoia a cathedral, drinking fog, which truly is Holy Water.

The snowmelt I drank in an ice cave: rights.

Those ghost-conversations of coyotes: rights.

That soul-blown sound of a train at night—part love, part loss, and part Coltrane—couldn't be more human, with the human right to quiet, so that everyone who needs to hear can hear.

And what about you? Isn't there a lakeshore somewhere? Or a night in some December? Or a time you saw some pronghorn and were doubly surprised—first by their nearness, then a second time by how they leapt away: too squat to be bounding like that? Isn't there a long-distance drive you've taken with a good enough reason at the end of it? Or a kiss that lives in your memory, that goes on rivering and rivering? Or a view from the porch of a lightning storm coursing the sky?

Anyway, it's April, soon to be summer in Utah, where most aren't yelling and opposed to helping refugees. Most don't think it's okay to zero them out, leave them trapped in their national horrors. In New Zealand they've granted more rights than that to a river, which ought to be an elemental lesson. Here's hoping it flows all the way from there to D.C.

∽

Even starlight wants water. Everything thirsts: otters and dragonflies, and pine woods we used to call our garden. Even burial fires want rain; it's a ladder for the dead.

Why a dragonfly?

To leave the air and be an island.

Why starlight?

After eons, to finally see its face. ...

I stood once under the sprinklers and saw them: spirits uncertain of this signal, this half-ascending, half-fanning across the field—should they climb now, or wait for real weather? I couldn't say.

You can make fire speak by striking a match. You can use the wind like a rope. But water will drought you, or drown you, or not; it decides.

It's a full song, water. It's a voice with no need for guitar.

Hold on, you're using three hands, not two. Start again at the beginning.

Out of the darkness, a river of light. Then cedars rose along lakeshores. And water was there, God's heartbeat, the engine of it all.

∞

What is the meaning of meaning?

A river.

That's it?

Well, maybe a wide enough one to skip rocks.

∞

I teach a Modern Legacies course at Utah Valley University. I call it "Futuristic Fiction: Paranoia or Prophecy?" I supplement novels with film clips and stories, pair them with Plato's *The Republic* and current events. Tolkien's *The Two Towers* isn't part of it. Wrong genre, for starters. Too many elves. But, damn, if the Golden Hall of Meduseld isn't a lot like Pennsylvania Avenue. And isn't the motive of Wormtongue exactly the same?—unchecked self-promotion. Think of what Tolkien's creep could have done with a gizmo as wormy as Twitter. Worse, our Wormtongue-in-Chief has Wormtongues of his own—*whisper whisper*—like Secretary Zinke suggesting, for instance, that too much land and ocean life are being preserved.

"My ass!" roars Teddy Roosevelt. He wads up Zinke's monuments report, yells, "Pull," and blasts it from the air.

"Good shot, Mr. President."

"I don't need flattery from suck-ups, Junior."

Then the spirit of Roosevelt exits. End of scene.

How beautiful would that be? The sun taking a last look back before setting, turning the Potomac to silver, and Zinke alone with his thoughts, whatever they are. I doubt they'd be this: *We ought to make the Grand Canyon smaller*. But I don't know for sure.

Here's something you might not know: Back in the days of its designation, locals opposed the Grand Canyon. "Strictly mineral country," they called it. This was when it was all just flatland. So they dug and picked and shoveled after treasure. They hoisted with pulleys.

Their pack mules hauled rock. But the only thing they uncovered was a river, and eons of useless view. . . .

It's time now to mention Montana—stepping down from the bus in Polson, nothing but an orchard between me and Flathead Lake. It looked like the Rockies were floating on the water. There's a word for that. It's *reflection*.

Or that spot along the Clark Fork River where the piling is topped by an osprey nest.

Or rounding a hilltop highway, bound for Great Falls, and openness everywhere, suddenly there, forever as the ocean, only green. All grass. No billboards. And the road straight out in front of me, up to the sky. Well, not really; that was just the feeling: so much and so all-at-once that I had to stop the truck. It was making my eyes tear.

And Secretary Zinke, you're from there, so what's going on? What's wrong with your vision? Are the tribes of Utah—past, present, future—worth less than others in your factoring? Imagine right now that I'm your teacher, and it's fourth-grade math; I'm saying, "Show me your work."

And imagine, further, that you're listening. Not tuned-out-staring, but for real: Pacific tuna will never recover, not if you "right size" Maritime Monuments, and "The Creator of All" means Creator of atolls. Of coral. Of moray eels.

Or imagine that Karma is a shark, and you're boatless, probably dead from thirst and exposure, which is maybe merciful and maybe not, depending on your view of the oceanic whitetip.

If you soaked the moon in napalm, lit it on fire, that's Northern Canada. That's the trading of tar sands for land and air, immeasurable in miles per gallon.

Sometimes I wonder what the future will think, assuming that people are a part of it. How many rpms on their constant question: *Why?*

∞

While the minutes hang between spring and summer, let's turn our attention to the future: What will it bring?—a thousand ski jumps? a rare gold panda? or just a river, two hills, and a bridge in between?

We could make that crossing. It would take less skill than a Japanese garden. And the sky wouldn't fracture, the clouds would still flower, so what the hell?

∞

Two things happened that got me thinking. This was during the Get Lit! Literary Festival, and I was staying at the Red Lion at the Park, standing out back on one of the footbridges, listening to the Spokane River.

Airports, hotel lobby, various conventioneers at various conventions, all in that fleecy-vest type of get-up, so maybe you can understand what happened: Out of the corner of my eye I spotted a man walking up, pulling his rolling carry-on luggage. He stops to fidget, and I turn back to watch the river pouring through the open floodgate. Then I catch him again, crossing the bridge behind me, only he doesn't have a suitcase at all. He's walking his dog. He's holding a leash.

Perception is crazy weird. Either the brain takes shortcuts, or it's trickable, or both. So that was the first thing.

The second is I'd gotten an email from my friend Jamie. He's the lead singer in a Steely Dan cover band in Seattle called Nearly Dan—good name—and I'd asked about his recent gigs, and he told me performing is a blast but that he misses the way we used to play music back in college. Meaning, on an actual turntable. We even had a sort of duel going, one or the other of us leaving a record spinning and a note saying something like "Drop the books, then the tone arm, and get your real education," or "Try to beat this one, dumbass," and it would be a lesser-known track from Joni Mitchell's *Don Juan's Restless Daughters*, or "Dangerous Type" off *Candy-O* for a kick-back four-minute flashback since we'd grown up listening to The Cars. The exact record doesn't matter, and it isn't the point. The point is that cuing up music on the internet isn't the same. Jamie was saying that in his email, and I agree:

Pandora,

Pandora is the roller-wheeled suitcase rather than the actual dog. It's misperception. And as a name, it's pretty lame and upside down because whoever made it up was skipping the facts: Pandora's Box wasn't a good thing, not unless you want blight to fly out and everything nice to be lost except for hope. Tactile connection?—gone. Design and aesthetics?—*whoosh*.

Intention, progress, and resolution?—voided out in favor of disconnected singles, then some others like synonyms, and so on.

She shouldn't have her name misused that way, especially not after the mythological whammy the Ancient Greeks gave her in the first place, the same bad rap as Eve: "Don't open that box, and don't touch that fruit tree. Just sit there and die of curiosity." Followed by: "Well, thanks to you two, everyone's going to have allergies now. And zits and mucous and cancer. They'll all stink, and struggle, and women will yell their guts out in childbirth, and people will be cursed with mosquitos and TV commercials and then robbed of their autonomy in old age. All because of you." That's a suck-ass story if you think about it, but I'll still take the original Tragedy over today's new Whatever-You-Call-It, with software doing your choosing for you based on stuff you already know you like. Maybe if it sparked curiosity, or if Spotify did, or the next thing comin' 'round the mountain, but nope; they just replace our curiosity with I-Don't-Know.

Q: What's in the box?

A: Just more boxes.

Q: Can I have a bite of your apple?

A: If I can have a bite of yours.

There used to be whole albums, these constructed sonic worlds, arranged in order and jacketed with cover art and liner notes. And sometimes those liner notes were like anthropological essays, or like eulogies for gone-away eras. Check out The Violent Femmes, for example: *Add It Up (1981-1993)*. Or Nat Hentoff and others on jazz recordings. Reading the liner notes on Charles Mingus's *Mingus Ah Um* (Columbia 1959) is how I was reminded about what an opportunistic, race-baiting creep Governor Orval Faubus was. If his name's not familiar, you can Wiki him, but I'd rather have "Fables of Faubus" spinning while I read from a record jacket I can hold in my hands. If I have to remember Faubus at all, or notice similarities between him and politicos these days ("Pandora, find me a present-day Orval-Eugene-type; bingo, out pops somebody yelling about Mexicans, Muslims, and women who aren't in his beauty pageants), then doing it via keystrokes or swiping would only make it worse.

But getting back to music—I bet you could tell Siri to sing Duran Duran's "Hungry Like The Wolf" and get something that sounds like an existentially sad Chihuahua. Or say, "Alexa, play 'Ring Them Bells' by Bob Dylan," and no doubt the song will play. But even so—even if you're sitting by someone amazing, someone who's never heard this song before—it isn't the same as lowering the tone arm, or opening the CD case and then the tray. ...

From that place on the footbridge over the Spokane River, you can see the dam, the open floodgates, colossal water pouring through and climbing the concrete banks of the channel, and it's pretty cool. But it isn't my favorite spot. The river is the least *itself* there and more like *somebody else's*. It isn't a whole album, just a packaged single. On repeat,

repeat,

repeat,

repeat,

repeat.

∞

It was the weirdest thing I ever got in the mail. It was from Annie, ten years after our divorce, and it was her ashes. From being cremated. And there was this letter with them, all official, stating she'd donated her body for hospital research. She'd died—"Auto accident. DOA."—and they had this form she'd filled out when we were still married, naming me as next of kin.

It was a strange feeling, believe me. Stranger than ghosts. First, you think it's a joke. Then you can't believe she's dead. Then you're finally left with wondering what to do.

So here's what I did. See, some things are more than an obligation, and I'd like to believe I got it right, just this one thing, anyway. What I did was split her ashes into seven equal parts; it seemed like the right kind of number: mythic and lucky. The first part I took up to Mt. St. Helen's. It had been years since it blew up, but that's just seconds in geology, and that was the point: I figured she'd be there for the whole rebirth, that she'd be part of it. From there I drove to Vantage, out on the bridge across the river, where the wind comes down the gorge at a hundred miles an hour. Her ashes flew everywhere, and I like to think they made it to the ocean, and Walla Walla ... Puget Sound ... and one day they'll wind up on a table in a restaurant where this couple is having some oysters, pasta, a bottle of wine, and right then he asks her to marry him, and she says yes, and it lasts forever. Then I kept on east to Polson, Montana, where the Rockies practically rise out of Flathead Lake. And the fourth part I went and scattered at Gasworks Park. You can see the whole Seattle skyline from there, and see the whole sky reflected in its glass. It's quite a place. And it's a quiet place. After that I went to Roy Street and left the fifth part in front of Bahn Thai. I love that restaurant. She'll get to smell that cooking every day. For the sixth part, I had to go back to Spokane and scatter them over the falls. She always liked the Spokane River, especially there. It would've been her birthday.

And that was that. It was all I could do at the time because the rest belonged in New Orleans. I needed to wait until Christmas, 'til the lights were up and shimmering on all the mansions and trees in the Garden District. It's amazing. Beautiful. Like what I think heaven will look like.

Assuming there really is one.

And that we even need such a place.

TEMPERATE COASTAL
RIVERS

Temperate Coastal River ecoregions are dominated by coastal basins in the temperate mid-latitudes. They are riverine ecosystems, but may also contain small lakes, coastal lagoons, and other wetlands.

THE WILD ATNARKO RIVER

Mary Woodbury

In early 2011 I was mapping beaches for a non-profit river stewardship program, my first job in Canada, and I came across Tweedsmuir Provincial Park, fairly far north from where I live. The description warned travelers that this area of British Columbia was isolated wilderness, rarely patrolled by forest rangers, and that people needed to be bear-aware and knowledgeable about back-country camping and trekking—and they should let people know where they were going just in case they disappeared. I thought to myself: but what if I want to disappear, at least for a little while—disappear from modern society. I had no idea then that I'd be making that journey in another couple years.

I had been studying the Great Bear Rainforest—reading all I could about its iconic spirit bears, salmon wolves, native cultures, and old growth forests. I was concerned by the then proposed Enbridge Northern Gateway—twin pipelines that would carry bitumen from the Alberta oil sands to the coast, where the oil would then be shipped in super-tankers across the Pacific to an Asian market. This project has since been overturned by the Federal Court of Appeals, which is great news, since it was an eco-catastrophe waiting to happen. I was still worried about grizzly bear hunts, mining, logging, fracking, and the increasing number of wildfires each year in BC. My research and writing about the area had brought me in touch with the threats to the rainforest, but also with what seemed like a beautiful paradise. I live in the lower mainland, a part of the temperate rainforest, but I was dreaming of heading north and disappearing.

After my husband and I talked about such a journey several times, we began planning a trip to Bella Coola. We would travel with our mothers and go on a grizzly bear rafting tour, along the Atnarko River, which runs through Tweedsmuir Provincial Park South. I'd finally get to see that isolated wilderness park I'd read about a couple years prior while hopefully being able to view grizzly bears wading up the river for salmon, and I was excited.

I just wasn't sure how to get there. The only way to reach the areas I wanted to visit in the Great Bear were by expensive planes or lengthy ferries. But Tweedsmuir Provincial Park is near Bella Coola, the gateway to the Great Bear Rainforest, and can be traveled by road, though a treacherous "hill" stands in the way.

What's more, having our mothers along was so important to us. A few years prior, I had lost my father to Parkinson's disease—a great struggle for me and the entire family, since he died relatively young and had been such a loving, kind, and patient dad and husband. Though my mom is a strong woman who picked up quickly after his death, without missing a beat—she had been married to my dad for several decades, and they had raised a family together—I was surprised at her constant strength to live life without him. She seemed to have access to a well of eternal upbeatness, though no doubt she silently grieved. This journey was her first big trip anywhere since his death. Mom was getting older too, and I just wanted to share an adventure with her. That she was so willing to get on the water where grizzly bears roamed was a total surprise—because all her life she had been wary around water. Yet, camping at Sheridan Lake not a year before, she had let me canoe her around the lake. Was she changing?

As noted, getting to the Bella Coola area of BC is tricky but possible. We decided to head from Vancouver to Kamloops and spend a night there—where my husband's mother lives—and drive up the next day to Bella Coola. This route goes through beautiful country, over eleven hours, or 735 kilometers, of small towns in British Columbia, increasingly taken over by wildflower meadows, majestic and rugged mountains, coastal Douglas fir, and subalpine pine and spruce. At Williams Lake, we saw a mama black bear and two cubs playing in a meadow. Not too far away, a Kingfisher perched high in a leafless tree, like a sentinel. Eagles nests, wooden fences, lodges, and cattle country marked the journey to isolation and what felt like going back through time—as if a portal had opened to a different world altogether. An hour away from Bella Coola, we reached the obstacle known as The Hill, also known as Heckman's Pass. The Hill is a dirt-packed mountain road on Highway 20 that has multiple switchbacks, and is 18 percent grades in some places. There is only room for one lane, with the uphill driver getting the right-of-way. It was late summer when we took this trip, so days were long and we felt lucky to have safely maneuvered The Hill before dark.

We entered a seemingly secret place away from time where mountains with perma-ice towered above smoke from nearby wildfires in the Coast Range Mountains. This juxtaposition played hide-and-seek in the light and shadow, with the sun's reflection setting the peaks agleam one minute and in the next moment, a ghostly mix of mist and smoke would drift across the mountains. Below snaked the Atnarko River, which flows from Charlotte Lake and runs approximately 100 kilometers before joining the Telchako River and Burnt Bridge Creek. Together they form the Bella Coola River.

After descending The Hill, we began to catch more glimpses of the river, which at times parallels the road, and western red cedars rose, providing a gateway to the wilderness beyond the road. The river cut through deep valleys, and its blue and gray waters reflected smoke and shimmering sunlight that occasionally managed to penetrate through. The river is reminiscent of past volcanic activity and is the home to wildlife such as black and grizzly bears, otters, cougars, red foxes, moose, deer, and mountain goats.

The road was by no means well-traveled, except for by a few—like the grizzly bear we saw at the side of the road, a herd of fat cattle crossing the road in its rightful open range territory, and, at one point, a horseback rider. Signs of civilization were lacking. Good! We were in the southern part of Tweedsmuir Provincial Park, and saw a sign to its lodge. The lodge was built in 1929 for hunters and anglers, and now is used by skiers and other adventurers. The lodge was closed when we visited.

We stayed at a different lodge several kilometers down the lone mountain highway. This facility also worked in conjunction with rafting guides, so we were able to arrange lodging and the river tour at the same time. The lodge itself was rustic, with lots of wood and primitive rooms with kitchenettes. The mountain home served us only for sleeping and preparing food since every other waking hour was spent on the river or hiking—or, in the evening, at a pavilion in a nearby meadow, edging the woods. There was nothing better at the tired end of each day than sipping a red wine while watching the smoky sunset, marveling at the isolation we felt and the magnificence of nature around us. The nearby fishing village of Bella Coola was just a dot at the end of the road, on the banks of the Bella Coola River, which empties into the North Bentinck Arm, part of a linked channel system to the large Dean Channel, one of the many branches of inlet waters from the Pacific.

If you traveled straight west out to sea, you would eventually end up at the southern end of the archipelago Haida Gwaii. During our stay, we rarely made it into Bella Coola itself, the home to about 2,000 people. We preferred the surrounding wilderness areas.

This slice of paradise up north is in Nuxalk people's (Nuxalkmc) territory; the Nuxalk have lived in the area for thousands of years. Many still live in the culture, and one of the weekends we were there, they had an all-night fish smoke. The band maintains their own fishery, separate from commercial fisheries, and they work to preserve the rivers, cultural traditions, forestry, and wildlife. In late August is when the salmon begin to swim from the ocean up the rivers and creeks to spawn. Coho, pink, sockeye, chum, and Chinook salmon come up both the Bella Coola River and Atnarko Rivers. And that's partly why we were there that particular late summer—to view grizzly bears roaming the river in search of salmon.

The rafting tour took place during a morning and an afternoon. I had rafted plenty of times before, mainly on Wisconsin's Wolf River, a great memory of my youth. We would rent rafts and pile in and scream down the rapids and through wild eddies. But the Atnarko River was silent and isolated, much like the wilderness around it. My husband's mom, who had driven "The Hill," and my mom, who had put away her childhood fears of water, boarded the raft first and sat near the stern, with us up front so that we could photograph whatever lay ahead. We had a guide with us, who spoke patiently and with reverence about the grizzly bears and other wildlife he hoped we would see.

I was nervous as we loaded ourselves into the raft, mainly because: who knew if a bear was nearby? We could see grizzly tracks on the gray sandy beach, along with fallen branches. We walk in their tracks. They walk in ours, I thought. What if we meet in between? And in the back of my mind, I couldn't help but think that if we saw a grizzly coming up the river, couldn't it maul us in the raft just as well as on the land? I had already realized, though, that our tour guide had been doing this for years, and nobody had ever been attacked. We just had to be very quiet and not make quick movements. The bears, after all, were not after humans—they were after salmon.

Once we were settled in the raft, the tour guide went over the basics about being quiet, respectful, not drawing attention to ourselves, and if we saw a bear to just silently watch it. We took off. One other rafting group was downstream from us quite a ways. The rafts were bright orange-red, the oars yellow, black, and blue. The gentle lopping of the water created a slow rhythm. Beneath the smoky skies, through which the sun tried to break, were the flapping wings of graceful eagles, hawks, kingfishers, and seagulls. Below us floated fresh-water mussels, which are muddy tasting. We also saw a few salmon, both live and dead—at least one a pre-spawn mort. On the river banks in a gentle breeze waved rainforest trees, wild flowers, and rose hips. We saw a grouse hiding in the foliage. Ducks with golden-brown heads and silver bodies glided alongside us. A sandpiper froze precariously until we paddled past it. The feeling was one of wanting to belong to this wild place. We had come to a forgotten part of the world where native peoples still relied on the ecological systems around them for food, shelter, and water and who were inextricably tied to this world both physically and spiritually—with no degrees of separation like we have in our modern world. How I wished I could move into this magical realm.

The paddling was slow and deliberately quiet, in respect of grizzly bears—who get the right of way on the river. We didn't paddle too far, even though we met early in the morning and did not get back to the lodge until late afternoon. We spent hours drifting and watching and being quiet. The guide told us that we should be very careful later if we chose to come back to the river, even on the banks. Aware of the danger, yet deeply in awe of the beauty of grizzlies, I realized that this kind of trek is not for the small-minded or disrespectful. Grizzlies eat a part of the fish, and the carcass left behind has nutrients that feed plants and bird species nearby. The connection among these species is invaluable, necessary. So this was not going to be a fast-paced raft ride among wild rapids but one where we reverently viewed the ecological cycle of life in the rainforest.

About an hour passed before we saw a grizzly bear coming up the river. The bear moved slowly, curiously, dipping occasionally into the water, but it was too far away for us to capture on camera without a zoom lens. I had only brought my video camera for a journalism class, and my husband had our wide-lens DSLR. There's only so much you can carry on a raft without being cumbersome. The tour guide whispered to be quiet. We all stopped paddling and watched the distant black shape shamble up the river. Its wet coat shone in the sunlight. I envisioned it coming to our boat, and my heart nearly stopped. But not out of fear so much as complete awe and respect (trust me, the fear and uncertainty was still there). It wouldn't be until a couple years later that I would view a black bear up close, not in a zoo or on the trail but in my own back yard—facing me down with a curious look—and that was white fear, curling inside, not sure if I would be attacked or if the bear would just run off. I merely went inside while it investigated some blackberries in our yard! But grizzly bears, beautiful as they are, can be aggressive. The grizzly stood up from its lumbering four-legged gait and glanced our way. Then it backed down on all fours and began coming up the river slowly. While I'm sure the bear saw us, it didn't seem to be very interested. It was nearing a fork downstream, and ended up stalking off onto the other fork of the river rather than toward us. We continued paddling, hushed, senses alert, but we did not see that bear again, nor any other bear that day. However, the rest of the river paddle was wrought with wonder: watching for more grizzlies, admiring the birds and trees native to the rainforest.

We went back to the river during our stay in Bella Coola and cautiously braved the river banks. We saw fly fishermen and other rafters, but the population of people enjoying this isolated area amounted to just a handful of others over the period of a few days. We were very careful as we hiked near the river, remembering that the tour guide had warned us that grizzly bears were very fast and we may not see them coming up the river. Running into us might surprise them, and if they felt threatened they might attack. I can still see our moms sitting near the river, a moment frozen in time. That picture of them is chiseled deep in my heart as I still remember how adventurous our mothers were, how my mom had somehow overcome her fear of the water, and how I wished my dad could be alive to see her sitting there with my mother-in-law, their hair lit by the sun and their bodies seemingly so tiny beneath the tall cedars. To share this experience with the people who brought us into this world seemed to be right in so many ways.

During our stay in Bella Coola, we did not raft again, but we did spot grizzlies near the river and we went, also, to see petroglyphs near Thorsen Creek. The creek is a spawning home to chum salmon and a tributary to the lower Bella Coola River. It is a show of respect to hire a Nuxalk guide to lead the hike along the creek to the petroglyphs. These rock carvings are five to ten thousand years old. The carvings depict animals and supernatural worlds. The day we went for a tour, an all-night fish cook had taken place, so the regular guide was busy with that. A younger guide led us up the trail along the creek to the petroglyphs, and once there, we met an elder who was cleaning off the rocks. He told us the amazing history of the Nuxalk and the stories behind various petroglyphs. We listened for about an hour, and though I don't remember the elder's name, he held our attention for an hour or so, his sparkling eyes and smiles showing that he was so happy to share his history with strangers. Seeing thousands-year-old rock art in front of us, and being tended to by an elder, was a magnificent thing to behold. His work, and that of the Nuxalk and other bands in the rainforest, show that acts of preservation are truly important.

Our journey to the gateway to the Great Bear Rainforest lives on in memory, and we would love to go back someday, maybe even deeper into the rainforest. Rafting on the Atnarko River, and spending days hiking along it, or nearby (we would just often find a neat place, park, and hike out), made me feel connected to the natural world in ways I don't get to do often enough, even though the lower mainland has pockets of rainforest that are somewhat hidden from urban life. I felt as though I had gone back in time, to an era before mass deforestation, consumerism, and habitat loss. I got but a glimpse of the wild natural world, of a wild river. That this journey coincided with being able to see my mother adventure again, find great peace, and show such spirit after my father's death—and that we shared these moments along with my life-time companion and his mom—bonded us in ways that are rare and rich.

I don't remember the drive back home. I don't remember arriving home. All I could think about for days, weeks, months, and now a couple years, was that time on the river and seeing the elusive grizzly bear, stately eagles, rugged blue peaks hiding in shadow and sun, large grizzly tracks on the sand, cedars touching the sky, the lazy river winding through time immemorial, and the stories the elder told at the petroglyphs. I feel like the Great Bear Rainforest is calling me back. And, yes, I would like to disappear once again into that surreal wilderness along the wild river.

LET THE RIVER RUN

Wes Ferguson

The Blanco River, in Texas, winds 87 miles through green hills and dramatic, rocky bluffs. It is dammed in more than ninety places, and a quirk in state law has ceded ownership of most of the riverbed to private landholders. They purchased it, and they pay taxes on it. But the Blanco is still wild. It flouts dominion. The river rises and falls, floods, and is redrawing its boundaries all the time.

Even modest swells can smash wooden decks and level stately trees. A family who enjoys a swimming hole for generations might find it filled with rocks after a single heavy rain. Once, I was walking with a property owner near the little village of Wimberley when he realized a gravel bar had hopped from one bank to the other. He seemed indignant: such caprice was an affront to his ownership. People who have known the river a long time are used to these changes, however, and they tend to get less worked up over them.

On a November morning in 2013, I met up with William T. Johnson, an owner of the Halifax Ranch, which lies on the edge of the Hill Country east of Wimberley. He was going to search for a couple of kayaks he'd lost in a flash flood on the Blanco ten days earlier. We climbed into his green Land Rover and rumbled down muddy trails beside the still-swollen river, stopping only to open gates at barbed-wire fences and to admire the damage. Flooding from the torrential storm had scoured the deep and narrow canyon walls of a dry tributary called Halifax Creek; the canyon basin seemed to have been struck by a tornado. Mature trees had fallen, shoved into enormous piles. The rock walls were chipped, broken, and deeply gouged. In the raw places where cascading water had knocked off large hunks of rubble, the stone was bright white, sharply contrasted by the weathered gray limestone around it.

"Oh, my God," Johnson said, looking through his binoculars. "I'm getting glimpses of stuff I've never seen. See that exposed rock? I've never seen that before."

Like so many flash floods in the Hill Country, this one had struck almost without warning. On the night before Halloween, the storm's bull's-eye had landed above Wimberley, several miles upstream. As 14 inches of rain soaked the hills that flank the southwestern edge of Austin's sprawl, the runoff surged into the Blanco and hurtled toward Johnson's ranch, then on to the small town of Kyle. Between midnight and 5:30 a.m., the river had risen from 4.3 feet to more than 35.9 feet at the flow gauge maintained by the U.S. Geological Survey in Kyle. The Halloween Flood, as it would come to be known, had been the town's worst flash flood in more than half a century—a mere 7 inches shy of the deadly Memorial Day Weekend flood two years later.

Sitting next to Johnson in his off-road vehicle, I stared at the destruction to Halifax Creek. "It's like a landslide," I said.

"Yeah," he replied. "Let's go to the top."

We left the river valley and drove uphill into rolling land covered in live oak and ashe juniper, commonly called cedar, its sweet, piney aroma filling the air. Wild turkeys gobbled as they darted across the road and disappeared behind stands of prickly pear. The trail ended, and we got out and walked. Johnson pointed to various plants in our path: pencil cactus, or tasajillo, with its bright-red ornamental fruit and vicious spines, and oreja de ratón, or mouse-ear, also known as Southwest bernardia, a densely branched shrub with small, hairy leaves like mouse ears.

Johnson stopped at a wavy patch of waist-high grass and ran his hand over the tops of the stems. "You know your grasses?" he asked. "That's the sideoats grama, the Texas state grass." Taking a closer look at the small, golden florets growing down the side of the stem, he grabbed the grass and pulled it from the shallow soil. I was reminded of our state flower, the bluebonnet, and the urban legend that forbids Texans from picking it. "You didn't just break the law, did you?" I asked.

We walked on, kicking our way through the grass. Almost without warning, the land ended at a rocky precipice. "Watch your step," Johnson said. "It's quite a drop." I inched toward the ledge, a balcony framed by pads of prickly pear. Nearly two hundred feet below, the Blanco swept around a sharp bend, a breathtaking swath of blue-green curving through a brown autumn landscape.

The water was deep but astonishingly clear at this spot, which is known as Halifax Hole. Every submerged rock and drop in the limestone riverbed was visible from above. "This is what I call the Great Bend of the Blanco," Johnson said. "Up until here, it's been flowing east. Here, it arrives and flows south. It's a major change of course."

We were standing near a barbed-wire fence that marks the eastern edge of Halifax Ranch. We could see the river far to the south, its waters still brimming. "Look down there," Johnson said as he pointed just beyond Halifax Hole. "Usually, if there's water at all, it's pretty modest."

The Blanco, he explained, is actually known to stop flowing downstream from the hole in particularly dry seasons—even as the river continues to run beautifully upstream. In 1912, in fact, the San Antonio Express reported a dramatic disappearance of the Blanco, when the bottom "fell out" of the river as water drained through faults and fractures in the riverbed. "There was a large body of water," reported the newspaper, "which unaccountably disappeared all at once, and there was not even a wet spot left. The fish were left high and dry, out of their native element—there was nothing to be seen, and all that was to be heard was the sound of rushing waters in 'the regions below.' "

This caused consternation among the people who needed a fully flowing river to power their mills and water their livestock, and so the owner of the Halifax Ranch at the time, a man named Mike Rodgers, hired a one-hundred-man crew to fill a "rent" he identified in the riverbed with rock and seal it with cement. But this ultimately failed to stop nature's course; Rodgers had overlooked two smaller sinkholes just upstream. So much water drains through them that, during dry times, Halifax Hole is where the Blanco stops flowing aboveground.

And where does it go? The subterranean river percolates through gaps, cracks, caverns, and fissures in the limestone, creating ever-wider passageways through which it moves, unseen, beneath our feet. In 2008 and 2009, to trace the Blanco's path after it vanishes from sight, hydrogeologists from the Barton Springs Edwards Aquifer Conservation District and other entities set up a research spot at one of the sinkholes, known as Johnson's Swallet. When they knelt by the surface of the river, they could hear and see the water draining into the ground. To chart its flow, they mixed some fluorescent dye in a plastic ice chest and poured the reddish liquid in the river. Then they monitored nearby wells and springs to locate the dye—which is tasteless, odorless, and invisible to humans once dissipated—where it reemerged from the earth.

Three months later, the researchers made a remarkable discovery. Their monitoring stations detected the dye more than twenty miles to the north, in Austin. It had seeped into one of Texas's most popular and revered artesian swimming holes, Barton Springs. In wet years, water from the Blanco is not thought to reach Barton Springs at all; the springs' primary source is drainage from six nearby creeks. But those creeks go dry sometimes, and during periods of drought, it turns out, the Blanco River is the single most important source for Austin's favorite swimming pool. The Blanco runs dry, but it keeps Barton Springs flowing.

Johnson stood on the bluff at the eastern edge of his ranch and pointed out another spot on the river even farther downstream. "That's beyond our property," he said. "It's what my father called the Nance Mill Hole." Johnson's neighbor, Scott Nance, refers to the same spot the Packery Hole. During the Civil War, Nance's ancestors ran a meatpacking operation at the site. "It's funny," Johnson said. "I have names for places, and he has different names for places."

There is also little agreement on the name of the ledge where Johnson and I were standing as we admired the view. "This is a buzzard roost, though they mostly hang out in the cypress trees or up on top of the bluff here," he said. "I've talked to kayakers who come by and they say, 'Oh yeah, Buzzards Bluff!' That's what they call it. I call it Decker Bluff, because it used to be the Decker Ranch. Old Judge Decker used to be the county judge."

Johnson's mother and father purchased the Halifax in 1933, and the Johnsons have added to it over the years. They now own more than two miles of Blanco River frontage. In this section of the Blanco, there are no human-made dams to impede the water's flow, and canyon walls rise up to two hundred feet above the banks. There are also very few homes. Dave Ellzey, the author of a series of guidebooks on Hill Country rivers, told me he considers the Blanco along the Halifax to be the second-most-remote stretch of river in the Hill Country, after the isolated Devils River (which many would argue is too far west to be in the Hill Country anyway).

Johnson and I drove back down to the river bottom and headed west to Halifax Falls, a series of three steps where the Blanco drops about eight feet. The crash of water echoed across the canyons. In his Blanco River Pocket Guide, Ellzey identifies this landmark as Triple Falls. "He came up with his own name for our waterfall," Johnson recalled. "I said, 'That's not the name of it. It's an interesting name, but that's not the name of it.'" The talk of names, their origins and conflicts, reminded me of the European explorers who identified so many of Texas's natural landmarks. Three centuries after Spaniards first encountered the Blanco and named it San Rafael Creek—it earned its identity as the white river after several decades of exploration—we were still debating place names along the waterway.

About a quarter mile upstream from Halifax Falls was a long gravel island whose contours had been molded by wind and water into dunes of red, white, and blue river stone. I'd later end up camping for a night on this island, the Blanco lapping the banks as a silvery half moon hung in the blue sky, and it would seem as if I was in the middle of nowhere—not 4.8 miles from my house in Kyle. Though some maps label it Paradise Island, it turns out that the Johnson family has never seen fit to give the stretch a name. The designations people bestow to various landmarks on his property mostly amuse Johnson, who has searched old county records in an effort to trace the origins of the Halifax moniker that's been applied to most of the features on his ranch.

"You've got Halifax Creek, Halifax Hole, Halifax Ranch, and various other references to Halifax—Halifax Cave, Halifax Falls—and we still don't really know where it came from," he said. "The first written reference I've found, looking at old deeds and so forth, was in 1857. It referred to the Halifax Cedar Brake something like ten miles north of San Marcos on the Río Blanco." He paused. "Well, that's here." Most of the area's first settlers came from the southern United States. The Halifax might have been settled by people from one of the Halifax counties in North Carolina or Virginia, or the town in the West Yorkshire region of England. Probably no one will ever know.

As Johnson and I continued our search for the kayaks, the Land Rover's tires crunching over more downed limbs, he kept an equanimous outlook on the sudden landscape changes wrought by the storm. "That's just the reality of living on the river," he said, "and I was starting to think it wasn't going to happen again. I was kind of shocked that it did."

At the base of Decker Bluff, or Buzzards Bluff, the narrow floodplain is rich with black alluvial loam that nourishes a forest of tall trees, including a state-champion box elder maple. We were driving along and admiring the view when we came to an unexpected dead end. One of the largest pecan trees I have ever seen had been torn out of the soft soil and now lay across our path.

"Oh, no! Oh, the big pecan!" he said. "And we already lost the other one, hit by lightning three times. This was our biggest remaining pecan. That's a blow there." He walked around to the snarled root ball suspended above the gaping hole in the fresh earth. "This I'm really sad to see," he said. "That was a healthy tree."

We never found the kayaks. After our tour, I concocted a variety of schemes to revisit the Halifax, and Johnson humored me, seeming to enjoy himself as we explored sites he has known since childhood. Johnson is sixtyish and tall, with fine breeze-blown hair, and he almost always wore the same pair of mustard-colored pants on our adventures. When he is not tending to his land along the Blanco, he runs an organization called the Burdine Johnson Foundation, which is named for his mother and supports the arts, historical projects, education, and other causes. (The foundation provided funding for my book.) Johnson's interests in natural science have dovetailed nicely with his stewardship of the ranch. Over the years he has opened the Halifax to biologists, hydrogeologists, and other scientists who treat the land as their two-thousand-acre research field.

Johnson and I spent hours during winter, spring, and summer rolling along hard-packed ranch trails, wading or paddling through the river, and climbing up and down brushy canyon walls. Tromping through vines and poison ivy, we traced the tinkling paths of spring-fed creeks to the headwaters, where they issue from cavities in the hillside. There we lifted rocks from the cool, clear shallows to spy on Blanco River springs salamanders, which can survive only in such microenvironments.

One day, to cross the river, we loaded into the Land Rover and drove along the north bank, tracing the ruts left by a frontier-era mail route, then turned and forded the Blanco at the base of Halifax Falls. It was the same crossing once used by pioneers driving horse-drawn wagons to and from the Wimberley village, thirteen miles upstream. Long before the arrival of Anglo settlers, around 1850, native people also used the Blanco River Valley as a natural passage from the hills and plateaus of the west and onto the Gulf plains of the south and east. The Comanche war chief Buffalo Hump likely crossed Halifax Falls before and after his unprecedented attack on the Republic of Texas, in 1840. As Johnson and I crossed the shallows, the truck tires sprayed water in all directions, and I imagined a thousand Indian warriors and their wives on horseback, trotting by the same waterfall.

We headed to the top of the bluff on the river's south bank, parked the Land Rover, then clambered back down in search of a dark cave where colonies of Mexican free-tailed bats make their summer home. When we found the entrance, I stooped down and reluctantly peered inside. Once, Johnson had told me, he and a party of cavers were about to enter when a feral Angora ram had exploded through the hole and gone tearing down the slope. Hearing nothing this time, Johnson and I crept onto our hands and knees and crawled inside.

This wasn't exactly bravery—humans have known about the cave for at least 150 years. During the latter part of the Civil War, it and others throughout the Hill Country were mined for bat guano. The Confederate army had run short of munitions, and the high nitrate content of guano provided a key ingredient in the production of gunpowder. Along with sulfur, the third ingredient was charcoal, which was produced by burning the cedar trees that grew in brakes along the Blanco.

John Thomas W. Townsend, a Confederate veteran from Wimberley, hired Mexican laborers to locate the caves and haul away the bat droppings. They filled buckets and used a pulley and rope to lower them to the river far below, where the excrement was loaded into carts and pulled by mules to manufacturing facilities, including one in Bastrop. Searching the cave many decades after the Civil War, Johnson's father found hand-hewn timbers inside. In fact, directly above the cave still stand two wooden poles that might have been used to mount the pulley system.

Not everyone contributed to the war effort, however. Even as workers were excavating guano at the bat cave, conscientious objectors who wanted nothing to do with the South's fight were waiting out the war a mile downstream in Halifax Canyon. "One of these evaders prophesied that the war would last for years; so he acquired some maple trees, no one knew where from, and set them out in the valley near his hide-out," writes Tula Townsend Wyatt in the 1963 history book *Wimberley's Legacy*. "His plan was to have his own sugar supply and after the war he would make furniture from the wood. A few of the trees were still growing in the canyon in the early part of 1900."

The author goes on to scold the nameless men who hid at Halifax Canyon and Little Arkansas, another picturesque canyon whittled into the hills about five miles upriver, for shirking their duty in the Civil War. "Perhaps they had not a pang of remorse for not having served their country in the time of need; but on the other hand, there may have been moments of hopeless anguish caused by a sense of guilt that followed them throughout life."

"A rare caracara flew above the trees at the edge of the river," Proulx continues. "Whitetail deer burst from every thicket. Our guide pointed out a barely visible horse-crippler cactus with curved thorns like a sail maker's needle. On the way out our host stepped on the brakes rather than run over a tarantula. We all got out and looked at it. It stood still, waiting for whatever was going to happen. It seemed handsome and young, about two and a half inches tall. A tickle with a long stem of grass sent it galloping into the brush."

I can picture Johnson mashing the brakes of his Land Rover to yield to the tarantula. About a decade ago, his family decided to protect most of the Halifax from future development by placing it under a conservation easement. In exchange for promising not to develop their land, Johnson family members receive tax benefits and will be able to enjoy their private wilderness in perpetuity.

Smaller patches along the Blanco are also being protected via similar easements, and conservationists hope to lock up as much of the riverfront as they can before the Austin-to-San Antonio sprawl overruns the Blanco entirely. Of course, time is running out. In recent decades, miles of riverfront have been transformed into suburban neighborhoods, and more subdivisions are in the works, with one real estate salesman describing the market for river frontage as a "Roman orgy on steroids."

It all reminds me of the words of John Graves, whose canoe trip down the Brazos River more than half a century ago paid homage to another changing waterway. Writing about ongoing efforts to reshape

Texas rivers, he declared, "We river-minded ones can't say much against them—nor, probably, should we want to." Even so, I am glad to know the Halifax will be spared such progress, a remnant of the Texas wild. And I hope someone is enjoying those two kayaks.

KAYAKING CHILE'S PASCUA RIVER

Diana Saverin

The remote beach was empty except for me and my companions. The broad expanse of sea was empty, too, and I squinted at the horizon, looking for a human shape. This was two years ago, deep in southern Chile, and five of us had just descended the bottom section of the Pascua—a burly, glacier-fed river—by kayak. We were at the Pascua's mouth, where it empties into a fjord, and we were planning to head through the fjord to the small town of Caleta Tortel. Two of the kayakers from our party, Lisa and Roberto, had paddled ahead until they disappeared amid the chop. Now, I was trying to find them in this gray-green world.

Seeing no sign of them, I walked back to the riverbank and kneeled for a drink of agua dulce—freshwater. Cold slid down my throat. The air smelled sweet, of mist and storms, and clouds were slung low above the water. Waves jostled and splashed, and I breathed deeply, readying myself for what I knew I had to do next: paddle through the tumult that Lisa and Roberto had just vanished into.

There was nothing for the three of us left on the gravel bar to do but load into our boats and point them toward the inlet. The other lives we all lived—an existence with things like showers and email and beds—had become laughably unimportant. Our needs were immediate and self-evident. Stay alive, stay dry, stay together, and keep going. Or turn back. But we had no intention of turning back. We gripped our paddles and pushed off the bank.

Where the river hits the sea, we hit the waves—heaving pyramids of whitecapped water that splashed over our spray skirts. My boat partner and I counted aloud to pace our strokes—one, two, three, four—as we dug our paddles into the dark water, hoping that if we paddled hard enough for long enough, we'd stay upright and make it to the nearest shore. Our kayak, about 17 feet long, rose onto the swells, hung in midair, then slammed back down. I clenched my paddle tighter. My forearms stiffened and ached. The land, the water, the weather—all of it became real and close. Although nerve-racking, this was the kind of intensity I lived for. It pulled me into the present and put all of me to work.

We aimed our boat for a beach that we could see between the waves. As we got closer, I spotted two life-jacketed figures pulling brightly colored plastic boats ashore. Lisa and Roberto had made landfall.

∞

Why was I there, paddling as hard as I could on those stormy seas? There's more than one way to answer that question. The Pascua is in a region of Chile called Aysén. I'd spent the past couple of years there doing research on a proposal to build five large dams, two of which would be on the Pascua. During the course of that project, I had learned a lot about river flows, hydropower, and electricity transmission lines. But I wanted to know the river that I had thought about so much in a more intimate way. Before the Pascua's power turned to megawatts, I wanted to feel its current against my skin.

I was also in Aysén for less practical reasons. Like many others before me, I'd been drawn by the idea of Patagonia: a place where wind and weather ruled, granite spires rose from the earth, and teal rivers curled through a trackless steppe. Parts of Aysén are practically uninhabited, with less than three people per square mile—a lower population density than that of the Sahara Desert or Mongolia. I'd hitchhiked through the region, kayaked its rivers, and explored its valleys, trying to get closer to the place I'd been so fixated on. The ecological philosopher Arne Naess wrote that mountaineering is a way to participate in a mountain's greatness. In the same vein, everything I did in the far south was part of my attempt to participate in the greatness of that landscape.

The Pascua encapsulates all that is wondrous about Patagonia. Other rivers in the area, like the Baker, are strewn with ranches, but very few gauchos—South America's version of cowboys—live along the Pascua. Those who do first arrived in handmade wooden rowboats. To get up the river before motorboats, the gauchos had to stand on the thickly forested banks of the Pascua and pull their boats (which were sometimes full of lambs) upstream with ropes. A spur road from the dirt highway did not arrive until 2006. The Pascua was remote, powerful, isolated—a force to be reckoned with. As a few friends and I talked about a potential trip on the river, we began referring to it as "the wild and unknown Pascua."

So, we decided that in February 2014 we would kayak the lower Pascua from near Lago Quetru to the shores of Tortel. Our crew would be Weston Boyles, a then-27-year-old Colorado native; Tyler Williams and Lisa Gelczis, husband-and-wife guides from Flagstaff, Arizona; and Roberto Haro, a middle-aged gym teacher from the town of Cochrane who taught local kids how to whitewater kayak. The four of them had met through an organization Weston started, Rios to Rivers, which had facilitated an exchange between some of Roberto's teenage kayakers and some American kayakers to paddle the Baker and Colorado Rivers while learning about the effects of dams.

Simply getting ready for the trip was challenging. There were no reports from other paddlers or even any detailed maps. So we huddled around a laptop in Roberto's kitchen, scrolling through satellite images to sketch a route.

Maps of the area show a shredded coastline where the continent encounters the sea. Islands are splattered across bays, and fjords slice into the mainland, carvings left over from the last ice age. Patagonia's topography is similar to that of Southeast Alaska and Norway, except with more places where glaciers meet the sea.

The journey promised heavy rain, cold temperatures, and high winds. Friends of ours could not understand why we would suffer through it. When we told people in Cochrane that we would kayak from Lago Quetru to the mouth of the Pascua, then up the coast to Tortel, one person asked, "Do you want to die?"

I struggled to explain why we wanted to go there. I often felt like using the clichéd response: "If you have to ask, you'll never understand." What drives anyone on this kind of quest? For me, it came from a desire to be part of something giant and wild, a yearning to participate in something beautiful. To do that fully, I needed to give up control.

∞

At the beginning of our journey, on the banks of the Pascua, we had packed our boats and loaded them into the water. The river was so wide, it often looked like a moving lake. Boils wrinkled the surface. The water split into braids around sandy shoals and bent sharply around unnamed mountains. We paddled up creeks and made sandwiches with manjar (Chile's version of dulce de leche) on our spray skirts. On our second day, we reached the Pascua's mouth, where the river emptied into the fjord and where our group dispersed and came together again on that wind-whipped beach to wait out the bad weather.

We took naps and ate snacks and read books, then eventually set out again. Frothing water exploded against cliffs to our left. To our right, the sea spread outward until it welded itself to a skyscape of gray clouds. No more beaches appeared on the coast. The headwind blew so hard that if we paused our paddle strokes, the Klepper went backward. I couldn't stop to scratch my nose. Weston and I synchronized our strokes. Much of the time, we couldn't see our friends.

After four hours of struggling against the wind, we ducked into a protected cove where iridescent clumps of ice emerged from the dark water—sedan-size pieces of glacier that had calved off from a tongue of the Southern Patagonian Ice Field. Most of the mountains had darkened by that time, except for one ridge behind us that was gilded by the only shaft of sun we had seen all day.

We paddled toward the coast, to where a few of these icebergs were beached on the front lawn of an abandoned ranch. Aysén is a ranching region, settled by homesteaders in the early 20th century, when border tensions with Argentina led the Chilean government to give away free land. Though more and more Ayséninos are moving to towns and making a living from tourism, the region remains a gaucho stronghold. These hardy souls live the life that many people hope will continue but few people want to live themselves.

We poked around the ranch—walking around the sagging fence that surrounded the cabin, pushing through the overgrown bushes, peeking into the shed where the family once hung their meat. Richard White, a Stanford environmental historian, has written that outdoor recreation like kayaking and mountaineering represents a type of "rugged play" that mimics the hard life of the pioneer. We gringos were trying to re-create the experience of those early gaucho pioneers—only we were doing it for entertainment rather than survival.

This rugged play demands that we use our bodies to move through the land until our thighs quiver and burn, our calves tighten and tire. It also demands that we look closely at whatever is around us: rapids and waves, discoloration and indentations in snow-covered ice, the outcroppings and contours of rock. We often feel closest to the land when it requires attention and labor from us, and so such play is a way of reconnecting to the earth. Among those of us who work with papers and pens, screens and keyboards, rugged play represents a kind of nostalgia. It's a yearning for the days when we knew the land the way the family at this ranch would have—when we knew it because we had to know it, when we knew it with our bodies.

My musings were swept away by the immediate demands of hunger, cold, and fatigue. We set up our nylon tents near the old wooden buildings, made fire and food on the beach, and slept.

We woke the next morning to wind hurtling over the water. The waves were even larger than they had been the day before. We set out, making spurts of progress up the coastline. I had a plane to catch in four days, but it was foolish to believe that we could control our rate of progress.

The next several days blurred together: a montage of driving wind and rain, Weston yelling at me whenever my hood wasn't up, and paddling furiously whenever the wind abated. We hung around on beaches when the weather was especially bad, then got back in our boats during the small openings when the wind died down.

One morning, we reached a beach at the tip of the string of islands we had been following since leaving the icebergs. The beach faced a seven-mile open crossing. The weather remained windy and wavy, with whitecapped water and biting gusts. There was no way we could head into open water in such conditions, so we waited again.

We knew exactly how much food we had left: two rolls of coconut cookies, two packets of saltine crackers, a bag of oatmeal, a bag of pasta, a few pieces of stale bread, and three bags of dried milk. The five of us shared half a bag of pasta for dinner.

The next day, the rains fell so heavily and continuously that Lisa and Tyler never took off their dry suits. The rest of us shivered in soaked-through rain gear, holding our pruney hands over a fire, taking turns gathering wood. At one point, Lisa and I walked to a nearby beach and heaved large rocks onto pieces of driftwood, trying to split them, joking that we'd become cavewomen.

None of us mentioned our hunger. We had chosen to give up control, and there was nothing we could do now but wait out the wind. We were all elated that night when Roberto caught a small fish. I ate the head—including the eyes. Tyler, who doesn't smoke, asked for one of the cigarettes we had brought as gifts for gauchos. He thought it would lighten the mood.

In the beginning of the trip, when optimism and awe had reigned, we'd fondly nicknamed each snacking and sleeping spot. Tranquilo Bay. Love Beach. We dubbed this waiting spot Desolation Cove.

∞

The next morning, hope displaced our desolation. Smaller waves passed by, free of whitecaps. We packed up our gear and readied our boats in silence, pointing our bows toward the lanky waterfalls and forested mountains that we could see across the open water. New snow dusted the peaks.

We crossed the previously treacherous passage with ridiculous ease, aiming toward a gap between the continent and an island. The seven miles passed quickly. We soon entered a protected channel, drifting by misty cascades and a curving coastline, enjoying

Roberto's secret stash of lollipops and opening up the two emergency rolls of coconut cookies. We were giddy with proximity. There were no more open crossings between us and Tortel. We guessed that we would make it to town that evening.

Midmorning, we spotted a gray wooden boat in a cove. Since reaching the mouth of the Pascua, we'd seen some detritus left from human activity on a few beaches—two deserted and collapsing cabins, empty gas canisters in the sand, rusty nails in pieces of beached wood—but this boat seemed to signal that someone was close by. A tin roof caught light between the trees. We could see chickens and dogs moving about, laundry swinging from a line, and smoke puffing from a chimney.

A couple stood outside the house, both wearing black rubber boots and baggy pants. We landed and walked up to their cabin. The man had a mustache, a hat, and a tentative posture. The woman had a wide smile and thick hair that fell around her ears. She exuded enthusiasm as soon as we introduced ourselves, ushering us into her house for mate, the ubiquitous South American tea sipped through a metal straw, and apologizing for the mess. They didn't get many visitors, she said.

It was a simple one-room cabin with a wood-burning cookstove in the corner. In another corner, clothes were piled on top of a mattress. Newspaper, pieces of cardboard, and a poster of the Virgin Mary covered the walls. A flattened cat food box was pressed against the door and often flapped, letting the wind enter. We sat shivering around the stove, swallowing mate, then bread, then rice, then fish. I was awed by the intense abundance; even the plate was warm. I went back for more.

We described our trip to the couple. The woman nodded. She told us that she'd grown up on the unoccupied ranch near the Jorge Montt Glacier—the ranch where we'd camped next to icebergs. She'd had to cross from there to Tortel many times as a child. It was the route her family had taken to get to town.

When we described Desolation Cove, she nodded again, adding that the wind always blew hard there. Once, she said, she had waited at that spot for seven days before she could cross the channel. Often, gauchos would wait together on that beach, all on their way to Tortel and all stopped by the wild winds of the open channel. Many would bring lambs in their boats for beachside asados. They would make tortas in the sand.

What many in Cochrane had warned us would be a lethal journey was, for the gauchos, just part of their routine. Our rugged play had once been someone's commute.

In the following days, after we reached Caleta Tortel, forces other than wind, weather, and water would take control. I'd hitchhike hundreds of miles to the nearest airport, try to weasel my way onto an interhemispheric flight, and apologize to my professors for being late to a new semester. I'd be quickly jolted back into a life of papers and pens, screens and keyboards, showers and email and a bed.

But those gauchos, of course, would stay, and often I would think of them: still there, watching the water, waiting out the weather, intertwining their lives with the land and paying close attention to its details. I was only a visitor to that place the gauchos call home, but paddling was my way of weaving the land and sea into my life. Beyond the picture of a place, the postcard version of it, was the possibility of participation.

PRODIGAL RIVER

Rebecca Lawton

> The river emerging from a dam is not the same river
> that entered its reservoir.
> —*Dams and Rivers: The Downstream Effects of Dams*

A sprig of dried plant lies on my kitchen table. Sent to me by my sister, Jen, the specimen has five sky-blue blossoms pressed flat and dried in a fold of paper towel. Leaves the color of green tea branch like monkey arms from the flower's pewter-gray, four-inch-long stems. Desiccated, mahogany-brown roots mass in a jumble at the base of the stems. The specimen is a wildflower, *Nemophila menziesii,* or baby blue eyes. Jen collected it more than twenty years ago in the Sierran foothills for her college Botany 103 class. In a letter she reminds me that I was with her the day she picked and pressed the flower: "We decided to take a walk up the north bank of the Stanislaus River. Remember? The water was low and the rocks exposed out in the river. But we weren't looking for rapids that day, we wanted wildflowers."

Despite the age of the parched specimen, it's clearly baby blue eyes. Petals of pale sapphire fade at the base, joined together mid flower in a central white eye. It's a lyrical plant with a lovely, cup-shaped corolla. When alive, the flower turned generously upward. It caught dew, offered itself to insects, and bared its delicate, shivery stamens to breezes. Jen's notes from our walk say that the hills above the Stanislaus were covered with the blossoms. "The flowers favor 40-degree slopes in sandy loam with surrounding live oak and gray pine forest." Among hundreds of such places, we chose one, and my sister set out a 20- by 50-foot test plot.

What had appeared at first glance to be a homogeneous patch of hillside among "classic yellow pine forest" in fact proved quite diverse. In the shade of oaks, we found ethereal surprises: fairy lantern and brightly colored fiesta flower. Ferns and saxifrage huddled in moist soil at the base of granite boulders. Out on the sunny slopes, lupine and grasses grew among popcorn flower and fiddleneck. Jen noted "a mottled mosaic of yellow and white."

Her test plot startled us both in its variety and wealth, like hidden treasure. She collected individuals of twenty different species of wildflowers from inside the plot and thirty more from nearby. She archived the fifty specimens as "a sample flora from the Stanislaus River near Parrott's Ferry Bridge." Recently, during a move, Jen came across the specimens and mailed the baby blue eyes to me with a letter: "I thought this might make you smile. Because of that hike so long ago, baby blue eyes always remind me of the river."

∞

During my first trip on the Stan in 1972, while I sat with a group of guides and passengers in a cool, huge limestone cave near Chinese Camp, I learned of New Melones Dam. It was the latest U.S. Army Corps of Engineers' dambuilding project. New Melones had by that time been in preconstruction for six years, situated dozens of miles downstream at the historic Old Melones townsite. The dam was to be 625 vertical feet of rock with an earthen core, a design like a jelly doughnut—dense material with a soft center. If filled to the brim, New Melones would back up nine miles behind the dam, creating California's fourth largest reservoir, with a surface area of 20 square miles and 100 miles of fluctuating shoreline.

I received this news in utter blackness in the Chinese Camp cave. "But what will happen to this canyon?" I asked.

Whoever replied had a broken voice. "Flooded. Completely gone."

No way, I thought. No one would deliberately destroy Eden. California seemed to have more than enough dams, and even as a teenager I had a sense of what we'd lose. There were just no other rivers as lovely and accessible as the Stan. By the early 1970s, its upstream whitewater run had become the most popular in the state. The project seemed as inconceivable as building the Pyramids in the middle of Main Street.

But time went by and work progressed on the dam, deep in a downstream canyon. Men with hardhats scraped hillsides clean with bulldozer blades. They diverted the river through tunnels in bedrock and dug footings with backhoes. My colleagues and I began to accept the building of the dam as inevitable, but we still hoped for a compromise with the Corps: a filling plan that allowed for water storage only as far upstream as the Parrott's Ferry bridge. This "build-it-but-don't-fill-it" strategy seemed acceptable to us—better than ruining the entire canyon. And it would meet the Corps' professed need for water, power, and flood control. The reservoir wouldn't be half empty, it would be half full.

The river hung in the balance as debate fumed over New Melones. A group known as Friends of the River materialized in a grassroots groundswell and led an effort to limit filling the reservoir. As a guide on the Stan, I took part. Each trip through the canyon assumed not only a bittersweet feeling but also a political charge. In our ammo boxes, we guides carried pencils and petitions to the state legislature, collecting signatures from California-registered voters at the take-out for river trips. On our days off from boating, we sat with our petitions at card tables in front of grocery stores in Sonora and Columbia. Or we traveled to San Francisco to stand on city streets and beg signatures from passersby. We must have looked a bit backwoods, young men and women in blue jeans and T-shirts. But we were effective. We needed 300,000 signatures to get on the ballot. We collected 500,000.

Next came public meetings, a push to get out the vote, and a whirlwind publicity campaign in support of our initiative, Proposition 17. Friends of the River drew on $238,000 in contributed funds to run a media campaign that consisted largely of radio spots. We were opposed, however, by a powerful, deep-pocketed coalition. They spared no expense. They saw our 200 grand and doubled it, funding such propaganda as a mammoth billboard at the San Francisco approach to the Bay Bridge that read, incredibly, SAVE THE RIVER, VOTE NO ON 17.

How shocking it was to see such deliberate humbug plastered across the landscape. Voting YES on 17 would actually save the living river. A NO vote favored New Melones, meaning the end of life in the river canyon as surely as if Noah's flood were to wash through. It floored me. Our opponents were lying—the evidence of it was clear even to my teenaged eyes.

∞

Baby blue eyes. They not only grew like weeds on the slopes of the Stanislaus, but they graced the banks of some of the other rivers Jen and I came to know. We found them on our visits to the American, Merced, Tuolumne, and Yuba. We found them on southern Oregon rivers, the Rogue and Illinois. Our time spent outdoors led us to train and hire out as boatmen for commercial trips. We became like human otter, spending all day every day on or near the water. Rivers held our full attention and devotion for years.

A diminutive woman determined to handle big boats, Jen was able to guide using a foot brace to raise herself on the rowing seats. It worked beautifully, as if she'd been born to it. She rafted high and wild water on canyon rivers in Utah and held her own on crews of rowdy boatmen, even leading trips for many years. Eventually we both guided in the Grand Canyon, well into our thirties, long after our family and friends had given up hoping we'd live productive lives. We were goners, tuned to rivers and seasons. Summer brought its hot, full trips scheduled back to back. Fall became a time of poignant separations and endings. Winter offered cold, long months in which we waited for the rivers to flow again. Then, each spring, ready to cast off our landlocked lives, we converged on the river. Often we began with an inaugural trip down the Stan, when it flowed strong and cold and the hills were draped in wildflowers, a voiceless constituency waiting to be counted.

∞

Unfortunately, reservoirs with all their benefits come at a great price. A dam changes everything about a river, flooding essential habitat for animals, inundating prehistoric rock paintings, submerging historical townsites. Trees drown where they stand. River silt and sand collect in oversized catch-alls, starving the downstream river of necessary surges of constructive sediment. Fish populations cannot tolerate the drops in water temperature that occur downstream of reservoirs, with disastrous results.

Californians can speak from hard experience. Here, dams are held responsible for decimating half of our native fish species and fully 95 percent of our wild salmon. With unstoppable drive, we've leashed water to the tune of 1,400 dams throughout the state. For decades, the undammed river was considered profligate, untamed—a "wasted stream," with falls begging to be harnessed for hydroelectricity, channels waiting to be fitted with locks for ships. Only the dammed river was considered a working river.

Turns out, the wild river is the champion of working rivers. It feeds a myriad of lives, from insects to ouzels to beaver, all part of an important creature community. It waters the floodplain, replaces depleted soil. It builds the very land we inhabit, depositing deltas inch by hard-won inch at the edges of continents. It flushes marshes and slices sloughs. Flowing into the ocean, the river creates a freshwater wedge that pushes into saltwater, nourishing the life-giving water chemistry at the end of the stream. Only rivers can carve out the deep, green world of estuaries and provide the safety of harbors. The river's glorious, generously given water flows to the ocean, replenishing the very fluid that balances our delicately balanced system of earthly life, as important to maintaining equilibrium on Earth as the mountains that rise from the mantle.

Nothing in a free-flowing river ever goes to waste.

Those of us who battled against New Melones will never forget it. Until the defeat of Proposition 17, I'd never really considered that liars could win. My mother always said that cheaters never prosper, and I'd believed her. So what had happened? *We* were the guys in the white hats. *We* were telling the truth about the place. In spite of our honest effort, or perhaps because of it, we lost the night of the election. Returns came in against the Stan, so fast that those of us watching didn't have to stay up late to know the televised outcome. The misleading campaign had worked. Later polls would show that only four percent of voters had wanted a dam.

After the election, the environmental battle raged on. Over more than a decade, river lovers tried everything. Led by Mark Dubois and Friends of the River, we appealed to President Carter not to fill New Melones. We brought a lawsuit against the Corps for its flimsy Environmental Impact Report. We tried state and national legislation. The ultimate act became the civil disobedience conducted at the eleventh hour, as waters rose behind the dam. Defying the laws that had cleared the reservoir, Mark chained his ankle to the canyon's bedrock at the rising river's edge. In doing so he protested far larger and irreversible infractions: the Corps' violation of a California order that the reservoir couldn't be filled, as well as a Supreme Court decision that confirmed California's right to limit filling. He spent critical days and nights chained in a secret place in the canyon as his messengers disseminated word that filling had to stop or Mark would drown. The nation held its breath until the Corps stopped the filling, then breathed a sigh of relief as Mark chose to leave the canyon.

Despite efforts to end the filling permanently, it resumed. Homesteads slipped under the inky, oceanic quiet of the waters. The Old Melones townsite went under, as did canyon walls with hematite-paint pictographs dating back eight thousand years. Riverside limestone caves submerged, with their underground sanctuaries big enough for a crowd. The showcase stalactites and stalagmites we'd taken pains not to ruin with our touch went under the dissolving power of millions of gallons of water. Protesters formed a human chain across the lower river to mark an acceptable upstream limit for the floodwaters. The water rose above it. Soon it became too high for anyone to safely stand in, and all we could do was bear witness.

Death by drowning is never a pretty sight, and the Stanislaus River canyon was no exception. Swallows wheeled in panicked flight at the Old Melones Bridge as water engulfed their mud homes, still full of nestlings. Small mammals, stranded by the rising flood, clung to the tops of willows and had to be rescued by boat. Water, normally a wondrous, life-giving substance, oozed into every dry cove, onto each warm patch of sand, into the nooks in every living tree trunk. Jen's plot eventually flooded. Whole forests drowned with it.

CO

Last week, remembering the Stan, I stopped in Santa Barbara, California, to visit a tree that survived the deluge. A gray pine, the tree was transplanted as a seedling from the Parrott's Ferry area of the Stan just before the filling of New Melones. One of the few pieces of riparian life to escape the flooding, it now stands at a roadside park a mile or so from Highway 101. Since its replanting around 1980, the pine has grown to about 30 feet tall.

One of several trees in an island park surrounded by suburban roads, the pine lives in a posh neighborhood. Its boughs reach toward the mountains, its needles catch the morning sun. No doubt its bark sometime glows red at sunset, as before. It is the only gray pine from within the original Melones footprint that's still living and breathing. Like us, it's a refugee from the wild river.

I'd rather my daughter—and all the children—could see the Stan's grass-covered hills and the wildflowers and gray pines in their natural homes. I still reminisce about that rich place, back when my sister and I could barely count the numbers of plants and animals that lived there. Jen's notes from our collection day say, "Someday, when the Stanislaus River is nothing more than a silt-filled reservoir, someone will ask, 'What was it like before the lake?'" And we'll know.

We have the gray pine—and the baby blue eyes—to always remind us.

⚮

Author's note: More than fifteen years have passed since the heady days when I completed my first solo book, *Reading Water: Lessons from the River*. A few weeks after September 11, 2001, Capital Books in Sterling, Virginia, decided to publish these words about wild places in general and wild rivers in particular. "These places are needed," Capital's editor Kathleen Hughes said. "More than ever." It was a courageous decision by a mid-size press in the waning days of print publishing. The world of literature was changing, as was the world at large.

Since September 11, our nation and the world have experienced more wake-up calls and tragedies: the sinking reality of climate change, the mega storms following on the heels of melting polar ice, more international war, America's gun violence, and the worldwide extinction of species due to human impacts. There is still so much to either lose or gain on our planet, and our very lives hang in the balance. Our need to integrate with the natural world to heal both it and us has come into focus more clearly than it did in 2002.

As a naturalist and writer who studies human and wild nature, I've seen and felt the deep effects of society's disenfranchisement from the earth: loss of community, imagination, and resilience in our towns, rural areas, and wilderness. And so I returned to *Reading Water*, to offer it again to new audiences as balm for our souls.

In the original release, "Prodigal River" contained some misinformation, which Tim Palmer pointed out in 2002 after we'd gone to press. The corrected version printed here notes that Mark Dubois left the Stanislaus River on his own authority, after the filling of New Melones reservoir had been halted because of his efforts. Mark was not removed by others.

I've learned from working in environmental science over four decades that hope for our planet is linked directly to our home watersheds. The rivers and streams that define us are critical refugia for diversity of biota and, therefore, genetic hardiness in a changing world. Each individual stream corridor is worth defending or restoring as we strive to protect ecosystems. Within our healthy aquatic communities, stream buffers, riparian habitat, and the very water column between the riverbanks, we find hope for the human race and our non-human counterparts.

In that spirit of hope, please dive into these lessons from the river—again, or for the first time—with optimism that it will endure.

PADDLING THE SEWERSHED

Brice Particelli

We splurged on the raft. While the picture on the box clearly showed two young kids paddling a placid lake, it also boasted a "motor-mount fitting" for an engine. It was comforting to know that this raft at least pretended to be built for rougher stuff.

My paddle-buddy, Cuong, paused in front of a cheaper one. "Are you sure this one won't do?" he asked. It had one air compartment and looked even more like a toy. "It's only $32."

We should have known then that we were in trouble. Neither of us knows much about paddling a river. We are friends through rock climbing. Cuong is a photographer and graphic designer, I'm an English professor, and we became friends through outdoor adventure—climbing in Central Park, surfing in Brooklyn, and mountain biking in Queens.

It's a ridiculous idea. We plan to paddle the entire twenty-four miles of the Bronx River, top to bottom, in two days. It's so ridiculous that there is no evidence of anyone even talking about doing it, let alone attempting it. Only the last eight miles of the Bronx River are officially paddleable (with a permit we do not have), and there are no campgrounds anywhere along the river. In fact, I'm not sure if any part of this trip is legal.

What we do know is that it's generally a bad idea to take a blowup raft down a shallow river. Coming from downtown Manhattan, though, we couldn't figure out how to get a canoe through the subway turnstiles.

"Let's get the raft with three air compartments," I said. "Just to be safe." Plus, at $44 it also came with a patch kit, paddles, and a pump.

"Okay," Cuong laughed, "I guess we don't want to end up swimming down the Bronx River."

We picked up a $21 camouflage tarp tent as well and a couple of days later we threw on our packs, took the subway to a commuter train and headed north to paddle New York City's last remaining fresh water river.

∞

To call the Bronx River "fresh" is a bit misleading. Through the nineteenth and twentieth centuries, it became a natural sewer for industrial waste. Factories, processing plants, and scrapyards lined the south, while up north, in the affluent suburbs, the Bronx was treated more as sewer than stream. In fact, until a lawsuit in 2007, the wealthy dumped their raw sewage into the river any time it rained hard. When you add in the runoff that happens when you cover marsh and stream with asphalt, you understand why the NYC Parks website says that they "commonly refer to sewersheds rather than watersheds in the Bronx."

I've talked my friend into this paddle in part because I'm interested in this bit of my city and its history, but also because we're always looking for a new adventure in this concrete life. New York City isn't exactly known for its outdoor activities, but there's a solid tradition of people pushing at those boundaries. Whether it's kite surfers fighting to open beaches to kites, rock climbers fighting off liability concerns in public parks, or volunteers offering free kayaking on the Hudson, there is a growing outdoors industry in New York. And while much of it is economically driven, some of it is also rooted in social justice—the belief that access to green spaces should not be limited to the wealthy. It's a push toward green that brings both the National Parks Service's initiative to open overnight campsites in Brooklyn and Staten Island—at the fairly high price of $30 per night, and also the Bronx River Alliance to push for a connected and free Greenway trail through the poorest areas of the city. For outdoorspeople who've found themselves in the city, it's an interesting phenomenon to explore. So when we saw a sudden window of warmer weather, we decided to give it a shot.

∞

The train drops us thirteen miles north of the city in the suburban town of Valhalla, where the Bronx River is a babbling brook among manicured parkland. It is late March, at the tail end of a rough winter, so the snow is still a few inches thick. It's an idyllic setting, with large homes on rolling hills, and the trails are sun-drenched and empty. We walk down tree-lined paths in old sneakers, pushing through the crusty snow, looking for deep water.

After a couple of miles, Cuong, who goes by Koon because kids in Michigan couldn't pronounce his Vietnamese name, is getting antsy. "This looks good enough," he says.

There are sticks and rocks popping up all along the shallow river. I hesitate, but finally agree. We pump up the raft on one of the snow-covered banks and step back.

Our boat is too small. While the box said "two-person," apparently they didn't mean two grown men with camping gear. They might not have even meant two adults at all. After trying a few options, we realize that the only way to fit is if we lay our packs lengthwise and straddle our bags.

Our weight dips us deep into shallow water. It's slow going, and we're constantly using flimsy oars to dislodge the boat from gravel bars to get into deeper channels. We're in one of these fast-moving channels when Koon lets out a yelp. There's a sharp stick barely below the surface pointing directly at us.

It's too late. There's a loud tear followed by air bubbles burping. We jump knee-deep into the frigid water and drag our limp boat to the side.

There's a four-inch gash through the outside bladder and our patch kit is useless. We're only a few miles in and we've popped one of the three air bladders that keep our boat afloat.

"I think we were a little overanxious to get in," I say.

Koon gives me a look that lets me know I've stated the obvious.

We decide to walk a bit further downriver to deeper waters, and head through trees and along train tracks until we reach White Plains, a shopping center town among the wealthy suburbs. We launch again, paddling under bridges and between buildings while people smile at us from above. The sun washes snow from the parking lots, funneling water into the river through plastic drainage. The brook is finally becoming a river.

"I've never been so excited to see street runoff before," I say.

As we head under a highway it's my turn to gasp.

Just under the bridge, hiding in the shadows, is the top of a sunken refrigerator—its jagged edge a few inches below the surface. We jam our paddles to turn the boat but it's too late. There is another horrible tear followed by the gurgle of escaping air.

We've lost two of our three bladders in the first several miles.

Without an outside bladder we're almost round, and now without a bottom bladder we dip low. While the water is deeper, every time we paddle now we spin sideways. We must look like a teacup ride in an amusement park—spinning back and forth, zigzagging downriver. And we're taking on water. The refrigerator punctured our boat all the way through so there are little pinhole tears that slowly seep water into our hull.

Koon, who has worked as a rock-climbing guide and is a gear-fiend at heart, is far more prepared than I. He has waterproof pants and a cover for his bag, while I'm in jeans that have swelled to six times their original weight. My bag is soaked and I'm pretty sure my sleeping bag is too. It is going to be a cold night.

We pass into Scarsdale where the riverbanks are lined with glistening McMansions and Tudor-styled cottages that each look like they could fit a family of forty. The river winds along private yards and town parks, past the picturesque brick and stone village. Any hint of trash that had begun to appear in the more urbanized White Plains is gone now, picked up by a vigilant town-funded parks crew. Scarsdale is one of the wealthiest towns in America, named the number one "Top Earners Town" by *Money Magazine*, and, along with Mount Vernon, White Plains, and Greenburgh, had to be sued to stop dumping raw sewage into this river. But the Bronx River also seems like a centerpiece here—a soothing vein of natural beauty—and we weave through the suburbs like we're on some sort of quaint amusement park ride. Lululemon walkers pass by without a glance.

I've been to Scarsdale before, to their public high school. It's an amazing place, complete with a college-level library, performing arts department, and tennis courts. I remember it as a stark contrast to my work at the time as a consultant for New York City schools. Both were "public," but the poorer city publics struggled to recruit teachers, pay for classroom books, or offer any arts at all. Many couldn't even offer basic health classes. They simply didn't have the space to let students run free. It felt tragic, to see this disparity under the same term, "public," and only a dozen miles away.

∞

As we head south, toward the city, the trees begin to disappear. The buildings grow denser. City lights turn on and roads replace trees along the riverbanks. The change feels swift, in part because we're losing sun and getting nervous.

"We need to figure out where to sleep," Koon says.

We consider a small island in the middle of the river, or a crowded cemetery, but we finally settle on an embankment under an outskirt downtown. There is a small floodplain of trees below a condo complex. A hundred feet uphill there is a bodega and a fast food joint, but the embankment shields us from view. A tree-lined highway buffers the other side. We drag the boat out and pull our soaking wet bodies onto shore. We are exhausted, and I just want to get dry, warm, and pass out.

"We need to be smart about this," Koon says. "We don't want cops waking us up at 3 a.m. with dogs and batons." He clears a bit of brush from behind a fallen tree. "This'll work. No one can see us from above, and hopefully cops don't look off to the side when they're driving by."

We're trespassing. I'm not sure if this is public land or private but I'm positive that we're not allowed to be here. Trespassing is a Class B Misdemeanor in New York, which could result in up to three months in jail and $500 in fines. People are meant to sleep in apartments and houses, not along the river.

Our $21 camo tent offers the perfect cover. The greens and grays fit with the brush, and the plastic fits with the trash. Even if you notice the tarp, it might just be a bit of plastic washed ashore.

We set it up and bring our wet clothes inside to keep them from freezing. It's supposed to be 34 degrees and my pack, sleeping bag, and clothes are all soaking wet. Koon's are dry. I'm tired and want to be mad at him for not talking through the gear, but mostly I'm just embarrassed that I wore cotton on a rafting trip.

We rehydrate our camp food and are halfway through our meal before Koon laughs, "You realize there are a dozen restaurants within throwing distance. I'm not saying I want to be at one, but it's sort of ridiculous."

I remember a girlfriend of mine who hated the idea of camping. She asked, "Why would I leave my perfectly good home to sleep on the ground?" The question doomed the relationship, but she wasn't wrong. Whether you're hours from a warm bed or seconds from it, camping is ridiculous. It's the intentional self-denial of modern amenities. But there is also something serene about lying close to the soil, even in a damp sleeping bag downhill from city lights. There is a simplicity that offers perspective on need and desire. There is time to breathe.

There's something important about it being so near, too. Historian William Cronon wrote a controversial essay called "The Trouble with Wilderness" in 1995 that traced our history of preserving the "wild" inside of parks. He suggested that we've built a fantasy where we live one life, in town, while we try to preserve a separate, managed, pristine wilderness. He suggested that to do so preserves "wilderness" for the wealthy. It sets up a system where you must pay to access trees and dirt. It is why charging $30 for the privilege of bringing your child to sleep on the ground under the stars is problematic. Thirty dollars for me might not be much, but for a family living on minimum wage it quickly becomes "something rich people do," and that seems wrong. Equally bad, Cronon said, the separation of nature and civilization encourages us to destroy those areas not "preserved." Cities become purely utilitarian—nothing but concrete, trash, and people.

∞

The sun wakes us up as birds chirp. This little oasis of water and trees has wildlife on it and we've become part of their morning routine. We heat water for coffee, pack our camo tent, and get moving.

Through much of the northern Bronx, the river cuts back and forth under the Bronx River Parkway, the Metro-North commuter train, business centers, public housing blocks, and apartment complexes. It runs with high walls on either side, hiding the water from city streets filled with more fast food chains, tire shops, and carpet salesmen than you could ever want in a lifetime. The river feels more as if it's in the way in these areas—something that requires bridges and winding roads, and it is filled with trash. What is most striking, in fact, is not the random appliances or tires, but the plastic shopping bags. They are scattered through the river like lost leaves caught on branches and rocks.

Near 211th Street, we reach the Bronx Park. This is the start of the Bronx River Blueway, the final eight miles of the river. Organizations like Bronx River Alliance and Rocking the Boat bring canoe groups down this final stretch, including local students who explore the river as a classroom. They organize cleanup and restoration projects, pulling hundreds of junked cars and thousands of tires from the river, and they put on community events like the Amazing Bronx River Flotilla Race. While tax dollars up north can go to parks, down here public money is more scarce, and slated for other things, so community groups and nonprofits have moved in to fill the void. It's all part of an environmental and educational revitalization of the South Bronx that tries to reconnect the river to the people who live alongside it. It is one of many recent and welcomed initiatives for a part of the city that has gone long-neglected. And as powerful as these projects are, they can only do so much. The last census report showed that this is the poorest Congressional district in the country. More than forty-nine percent of children live below the poverty line. In New York City.

The 718-acre Bronx Park is at the heart of the Bronx. Soon after the park was opened in 1884, the city allocated 250 acres to the New York Botanical Society and another 250 acres to the New York Zoological Society. That means that 500 of the 718 acres, then, are pay-to-play parks. In the poorest of districts, there is a massive park that only the wealthy can enter.

The trash slowly dwindles as we get closer to the Botanical Garden boundary. The river becomes greener and less covered in plastic bags. We paddle around a corner and see a small furry animal digging into a garbage bag on a branch over the river. "Is that a beaver?" I ask. His nose is down so I can't quite make him out. "—or a rat?"

He pulls his head up and looks directly at us.

"That's a beaver," Koon says, jumping up from his pack with such excitement that I worry we'll tip.

In 1997 the first beaver in more than 200 years was spotted on this river. During the time of the Mohegans, when this river was called the Aquehung, or "River of High Bluffs," locals relied on small game like beaver and fish for food. When the Swedes and Dutch arrived in the early seventeenth century, they lived as trappers until they hunted the land bare. They built mills and factories next, as the industrial era took hold, and the fish were polluted out of the river.

It was a big deal when the first beaver came back, so they named him Jose after a South Bronx Congressman who helped find funding for river restoration. A second beaver recently joined Jose, and from the pictures I've seen, this looks like that second, nameless one. It's a good sign for a once-dead river.

As we get deeper into the park, we reach a low bridge with a security camera pointed at the water. There are so many railings and wires that I back-paddle for a moment.

"You think it's alarmed?" Koon asks. "We don't exactly have the right permits."

"It looks more like a booby trap."

"I guess there's only one way to find out," Koon laughs.

We paddle through without alarm and soon see people walking along the wooded paths, snapping pictures of trees and birds and us. They smile and wave and as we get closer a young couple stops with their boy.

"Where are you guys going?" the mother asks.

"To the East River," I say.

"Really? They're paddling all the way down to Manhattan," she tells her son. "How far is that?"

"Seven more miles."

"Good luck!" the boy yells.

There are three portages through this park—dammed parts of the river where we'll have to walk the boat around on private parkland. We reach the first and carry the boat down a thin road, past a small dam where the water cascades across a rough patch of ledges and mini-waterfalls, and then past an old Dutch stone mill.

A golf cart with two maintenance guys comes over the hill toward us.

"Is this going to be a problem?" Koon asks me.

I have no idea so I offer them the friendliest wave I can.

"Nice day to be out here," one of the guys says, unfazed.

"They don't seem to care," Koon laughs.

We head down a dirt path just as a police cart comes over the hill.

"Hurry up," Koon says, and we dip out of sight.

Past the first dam, the water opens up to a horizon filled with herons and egrets. There isn't a single road or building in sight. It is serene and we might as well be a hundred miles away. Or four hundred years ago. We chase a flock of ducks downriver until the Fordham Road overpass, the roadway that separates the Botanical Garden from the Bronx Zoo.

On our first portage inside the Bronx Zoo we have to cross a pair of tall waterfalls among deep woods. The path around the falls is short, and we're only on parkland for a moment. We begin to paddle away when we see two security guards on the other bank of the river pointing at us. One walks toward us, but he is on a ridge twenty feet above.

I yell a hello over the raging waterfalls.

"How'd you guys get around those waterfalls?"

"There's a path," Koon says. "We just carried the boat around."

The guard smiles and watches us paddle past.

The river is widest through the Zoo and the long horizons let us realize how slowly and erratically we're paddling, shimmying down this broad river with each paddle turning our teacup boat sideways. We paddle under the Wild Asia Monorail, which carries passengers through Mongolian Horses, Asian Elephants, Red Pandas, and Bengal Tigers. Just past, a tiny head pops out of the water. It's another beaver, twice as big as the first. This, I want to assume, is Jose.

"I can't believe there are beaver here," Koon says.

We're in the center of Bronx but it's the very picture of sublime, as if we've invaded a Hudson Valley School painting. Waterfowl fly above and there are nothing but trees on either side. We're alone here. The river in front of us seems to end at the horizon as if we could be paddling in silence for miles more to come.

We turn a corner and the serenity ends as quickly as it began. There's a dam followed by 180th Street and rows of tenements. The dam is our third portage in the park and it's under construction. There's a tiny park on the other end that is getting a facelift, but the main purpose of the construction is a new fish ladder—a set of water-filled steps that allow fish to make it over the dam. The Park's Service has begun reintroducing Alewife and Blueback Herring to the river, starting with the heartiest of species.

With the fences across the river and park, our portage includes climbing a spiked fence and walking across 180th Street. We pass our gear and boat over a piece at a time, careful to keep from impaling our fragile boat—or ourselves—on the long metal spikes.

Across the street, the riverbanks are made of a hundred yards of car tires, stacked eight feet high and holding back the land that carries the weight of a dozen tenements that seem like they're falling apart in peeling paint and water-damaged walls. While the trash had slowly accumulated from the suburbs to the city in direct relation to the wealth of the area, here it is abrupt. Striking.

A woman is sitting in a garbage-strewn yard nearby. The building behind her looks condemned, crumbling into the river, but there is laundry hanging from a string outside the windows. She smiles at us, "That looks like fun. Can I come?"

"I wish," Koon laughs. "Look at how small this boat is."

The river is contained as far as we can see, funneled by tire walls, then rocks and cement. It is city drainage, and we're to be flushed out for these last few miles. We paddle past a submerged engine block, plastic bags, discarded clothing, and tires piled as plentiful as rocks. A swelled sock catches onto my paddle.

The buildings here are often boarded or dilapidated. Under each of the next two overpasses there are homeless encampments. We startle one man who is trying to go to the bathroom in peace.

The South Bronx wasn't always as poverty-stricken. Until the 1950s and '60s it was filled with middle class neighborhoods and factory jobs. Over the course of a few years, city planner Robert Moses cut up the Bronx with highways, using eminent domain to displace hundreds of thousands of people, cutting the population of the South Bronx by more than half in less than a decade. Moses wanted to make Manhattan more car-friendly so that certain people could live in the northern suburbs and drive to work downtown. He was at the forefront of a global urban initiative to partition each urban area into separated sections of work, home, industry, and poverty. Industry would be in one area, poverty in another, white collar work in another, and the upper- and upper-middle class would live on the outskirts of it all, in the suburban counties to the north and east. His mission was a devastating one for this area in particular. He gave many of those displaced families thirty days' notice to leave their homes before they would be bulldozed for highways, and he drained the city's public transportation funds to pay for it. As Moses famously said of his work here, he "took a meat axe to the Bronx." And while our understanding of city planning has shifted since then, the damage done has been written across this landscape.

∞

We paddle south through Starlight Park—a recently renovated set of athletic fields. The river is straight and contained and we pass a half-dead tree that hangs over the river. There is a rope swing dangling from it and the grayness of it all feels like a horror movie.

"There was a kid who drowned in a swimming hole near here," I say to Koon. "I wonder if this is it."

"Oh God, I hope not."

But it must be. There are trash bags and tires and broken glass but this is the only place we've seen that resembles a swimming hole.

I remember my own swimming holes, visiting family in Kentucky, where I'd flinch when my feet hit sticks on the soupy clay bottom. I wonder what kids' threshold for flinching must be here. At the same time, I also know that if I'd grown up here I would be the first to jump in. A swim is a swim is a swim, after all, and we all get used to our own normal.

We paddle past pockets of park that stand out like wildflowers breaking through a sidewalk crack. These parks have been popping up over the past few decades as community groups pressure city, state, and federal governments to increase park access to the area, asking why all of the parks are in wealthy areas, and wondering openly about the effects of Moses' meat axe. "Economic degradation begets environmental degradation, which begets social degradation," offered Majora Carter, the founder of Sustainable South Bronx, in a TED talk.

We can only wonder what kind of normal our society's children are growing up in.

∞

We head under a railroad bridge where two kids yell down at us, "You can do it!"

We're three miles from the bottom, shimmying back and forth as quickly as the slow river will take us.

An older man with dreadlocks sits on the steps of a park, smoking. He yells a hello and we wave back. He's in the Concrete Plant Park—a big grass field pocked with orange-painted remnants of a reclaimed factory, standing like sculptures against the elevated railroad tracks and highways. The city removed 32,000 tons of contaminated soil to make this park safe for use.

"Everyone's been so nice," Koon says. "We've never heard anything but positive things this whole way." And it's true.

"I wonder what would have happened if we were black or Latino or Middle Eastern?" I ask.

"We wouldn't have made it five miles," Koon laughs. "We probably would have been arrested before leaving Valhalla."

The river widens through warehouses and factories while big box public housing units and apartment complexes rest silently on the horizon. Row houses and brownstones hide behind highways and elevated tracks.

This is the land that Jonas Bronck bought from the Mohegans in 1639—over 500 acres stretching from what's now the Bronx River to the Harlem River, from 150th Street to the East River. According to the book *South Bronx Rising*, the land cost him "two guns, two kettles, two coats, two adzes, two shirts, one barrel of cider, and six bits of money."

Bronck described his new land in a letter home,

The invisible hand of the Almighty Father, surely guided me to this beautiful country, a land covered with virgin forest and unlimited opportunities. It is a veritable paradise and needs but the industrious hand of man to make it the finest and most beautiful region in all the world.

Bronck died four years after arriving but his name stayed with the river, Bronck's River, and the river gave its name to the borough when it joined New York City in 1898.

The river is wide here, at least a hundred yards in sections, and placid. We paddle past soot-covered factory buildings, a scrapyard, and along rusty barges. Above, there are railroad tracks and a maze of highways.

"There were seashells about a mile back, right?" I ask Koon. "After that last portage?"

He nods.

"I wonder if we're tidal now. Taste the water. See if it's salty."

"I'm not tasting this water," he laughs. "Are you crazy?"

There is an oily sheen to the black water.

"No, I don't think I would eith—"

"Ok, fine." He dips his fingers into the river and puts some in his mouth.

I cringe.

"Hm... Salty," he laughs, "but that could be my fingers. Plus it's oily. And cold."

He spits a few times but can't get the grease off his tongue.

We paddle around the next bend and see a massive garbage boom—a big plastic arm stretched across the river to catch the garbage. It is a hundred yards of trash, end to end.

To portage, we climb a rusty fence, and then pass our gear through a rusted-out hole in a metal wall. Our hands and clothes are red as we push off again, wiggling back and forth through the oily water.

We're probably going faster now but the long horizon makes our boat feel small and slow and we feel every wiggle. The shore is now a hundred yards away on either side when I remember that our inflatable boat is filled with holes. "If that last bladder pops, we're done," I laugh.

It doesn't. We turn the corner and can see the East River ahead. I pull out my phone to call Lauren, a friend with a car who was planning to meet us at the New Fulton Fish Market. She says that the dock is closed and she can't find a place to pick us up. There is nothing but fencing and food processing plants here, she says. I see a small gap in the fence at a wholesale grocer and I ask her to meet us there.

We paddle over. The shore is covered in seagull droppings, seashells, and barnacles, but we are no longer worried about adding holes to the boat. We drag it onshore and walk up toward a parking lot filled with tractor-trailers. While Koon pulls our gear out of the boat, I walk toward the road to wave Lauren down.

"I was just here," she says. "The security guard kicked me out."

We take a photo with our boat like it's a trophy.

It is an anticlimactic end, standing in a parking lot, covered in mud and rust and an assortment of other things I'd rather not consider.

We hop in the car and Lauren rolls down the windows. She is nice enough to not mention our smell.

As we drive away, the security guard walks out and toward us, arms raised. I lean out the window to explain but Lauren doesn't slow down.

"We're leaving," Lauren yells as we drive past.

I can only imagine what it looks like to the security guard: A woman drives in and is kicked out. Then she drives in again and when she leaves, she has two mud-covered men in her car.

The guard continues walking toward where we'd come from, toward the river. She looks at the trash bins, at the back of the loading docks, and at the rows of truck containers, but never at the river. She looks perplexed, probably wondering where these two men had come from. One of the containers? Should she call the police? Or send the surveillance footage to Homeland Security?

The river probably never crosses her mind.

She shakes her head as we head out of the lot, turn the corner, and are gone.

WHEN A RIVER IS A PERSON

Gary Wockner

Rivers are made of water, and water comes from rain, and boy, did it rain.

We came to New Zealand in early 2018 and just happened to hit one of the rainier summer periods in local memory. It rained so much that the day before our three-day canoe trip on the Whanganui River the federal government shut down the river to recreational canoeing. And then it rained so much on the first day and night of our trip that the government shut it down again, stranding us in a hut on the riverbank. As we waited out the rain, massive trees and logs raced down the waterway, as did several dead goats and sheep.

The river was swollen, running fast, and *alive*.

How appropriate for the Whanganui, the first river on earth to gain 'personhood' status.

The Whanganui is the longest navigable river in New Zealand, and its water and the land around it have been at the center of one of the longest legal battles in New

Zealand history. In March of 2017, the Maori people living around the Whanganui River won the battle. The legal victory gave 'legal personhood' status to the river, allowed the Maori to designate a person to represent the river in court actions, and included land-settlement negotiations as well as a large financial settlement for the tribes in the area.

The night before our canoe trip departed, we had dinner with our outfitter-hosts in the tiny town of Owhango. Owhango Adventures also runs 'cultural guided river trips' on the Whanganui. The meal was excellent—beef, potatoes, salad, and corn on the cob—and was prepared by Maori sisters Dianah and Maki Ngarongo, who work with the outfitting company and cultural river tours. After dinner, Dianah and Maki told us the compelling story of how the river gained personhood status as well as the moral philosophy that drives the Maori's claim on the river and the landscapes around it.

Dianah is often a spokesperson representing the upper stretch of the river. Her warm, eloquent words came from the heart. She welcomed the idea that I could help 'tell the story to the world' as she spoke of the feminine power of the Maori women who live along the river. She told us 'the women are strong on the river,' and indeed she has been one of the strongest and most outspoken leaders. 'We want the water and river in its natural state; we want to live sustainably on the river', she said.

The next morning, Dianah and Maki joined us at the put-in and sang a Maori prayer that welcomed us to the river. Our self-guided canoe trip began as we slid into a small tributary and then met the Whanganui a hundred yards downstream. Joining me in three canoes were my partner, and friends, many of whom are 'Waterkeepers' on our respective rivers and work with the international Waterkeeper Alliance to protect waterways across the world. We were thrilled to be paddling on the Whanganui, and to experience first-hand the river that has become a person.

The stretch of the upper Whanganui is a narrow canyon with rock walls and steep jungle forest careening down to the river. The rains had brought dozens of large waterfalls to life, their clear water crashing down the canyon walls into the muddy, swollen waterway. We raced along in the fast water mesmerized by the massive ferns, waterfalls and forest canopy. A sprinkle of rain joined us almost all of the first day but failed to dampen our spirits as we paddled into the John Coull Hut in late afternoon.

During the day of paddling, we hardly saw another person, but as we arrived at our destination, about 40 canoeists steadily streamed into the campground and the sleeping hut. The evening was filled with food and laughter as the rains came down harder and harder. It poured all night long, and as morning broke, the hut manager told us the Whanganui, had again shut down the river to recreational canoeists. We relaxed in camp all day, enjoying the company of international travelers and gawking at the flow of the river—which had risen over two meters overnight—as well as the massive trees and logs racing down with it.

Part of the river is encompassed by Whanganui National Park in the southwest corner of the North Island, and it's heavily protected and regulated by the New Zealand government. The Whanganui is a busy tourist river, with the upper stretch open to canoeing and the lower stretch open to jet boat tours that speed large numbers of tourists up and downstream.

New Zealand has a law called the Water Conservation Order that is similar to the U.S.' Wild and Scenic Rivers Act. The Order protects fifteen rivers across New Zealand, but the Whanganui is not included in that list. Although the Whanganui has been considered for this type of federal protection, the legal settlement with the Maori took precedence and now protects the Whanganui by a different mechanism. The Whanganui is also not completely free-flowing due to a few small dams in its upper headwaters.

Day three on the river brought sun and more paddling as the government opened the river back up to canoeing. Although the flow had not decreased, the debris on the river had disappeared. As we pushed off into the flow, we were whisked downstream as if on a jet boat ourselves. We relaxed and gawked at even more waterfalls as we paddled back and forth in the canyon to stay in the warm sun. Our second night on the river was supposed to be at a hut operated by the Maori, called the 'Tieke Kainga'.

As our three-day adventure ended at the take-out near Pipiriki, we were picked up and taken back to Owhango. We had dinner that night and mused about the rain and the swollen muddy river, and discussed the legal settlement and ongoing negotiations between the Maori and the New Zealand government.

The situation on the Whanganui is legally and politically complex, and it would be ill-advised to think of it as some sort of pristine native victory. The Maori have been fighting for 175 years to get their land and water rights, and that fight has been filled with conflict and controversy amongst themselves as well as with the New Zealand government. As Dianah told us a few nights earlier, 'This is not about an exotic tribal situation. We want self sufficiency, self reliance, self determination. We lost a lot of ancestors over the history of this fight. There's a lot of bureaucracy. But we're moving in the right direction.'

As the legal status and protection for the Whanganui moves forward, river conservationists around the world should look to it as an example, but also know and prepare for complex, controversial and long-term battles. We must do our work now, but it is likely our grandchildren who will see and feel the success of our efforts.

CATFISH BEND

Lisa Knopp

As a child, I didn't know where the Mississippi River
came from or where it went after it flowed past my
hometown, Burlington, and my mother's home-town,
Keokuk, forty miles downstream. Nor did I know that
Iowa's eastern border, as drawn by the Mississippi,
could be seen as a misshapen face and neck, with
Clinton near the tip of the bulbous nose, the Quad
Cities at the nostril, Burlington at the top of the lower
lip, and Keokuk on the Adam's apple. Nor did I know
anything about those who had lived at my bend of the
river before my ancestors arrived there. But I did know
how the river smelled, how an abundance of wriggling,
gasping, flapping, or snapping creatures lived near or
in it, how it shimmered in the sunlight or turned dark
when the sky was overcast, how viciously it could flood,
and how it oriented me in space, since the river was
always east.

I know now that Burlington and Keokuk had their origins in June of 1832, when the U.S. government forced the Sauk, Meskwaki (Fox), and Ho-Chunk (Winnebago) to surrender a strip of land about forty miles wide along the west side of the Mississippi, extending from what would become the Iowa-Missouri state line almost to the Iowa-Minnesota state line. Saukenuk, on the east side of the river eighty-five miles north of Burlington, had been the principal town of the Sauk nation. The several thousand people who lived there had cultivated some eight hundred acres of corn and other vegetables and had caught an abundance of fish near the confluence of the Rock and Mississippi rivers.

In 1832, the United States opened the Black Hawk Purchase to nonnative settlement. The next year, those who settled at the lower-lip-like bend in the river named their village Flint Hills, the English translation of *Sho-quo-quon,* which is what the Meskwaki called the place where they gathered flint for their arrowheads. In 1834, John B. Gray, who purchased the first lot in Flint Hills, renamed the settlement after his home place, Burlington, Vermont. There were other, more evocative names for my hometown, including Porkopolis (in the mid-nineteenth century, Burlington boasted three pork-packing plants), Turd Town (so named because of the contents of the Hawk-Eye Creek, which cut across town to the river), and my favorite, Catfish Bend. The latter is still an honorable name even though in 2007 it was appropriated by a casino that floats not in the river but in a pool of water near the intersection of U.S. Highways 34 and 61.

Catfish was a staple at our house. For most Saturday suppers my mother fried catfish in a flour or cornmeal batter and tossed a salad (potato, pea, cabbage, or macaroni) in a mayonnaise dressing. Cold catfish made a good snack, though my grandfather told me that I shouldn't eat fish alone. "Have crackers or a hunk of bread with it," he advised. Sometimes we went to the Riverview Restaurant in Dallas City, Illinois, a smorgasbord with heaps of fried catfish, or the Eagles Club in Burlington, which my mother judged to have the best catfish that she'd ever eaten and so big that the fish hung over the edge of your plate. Though my father fished, my parents also bought fish at Vice's Fish Market upriver in Oquawka, Illinois. Once, they were there early enough to see the commercial fishermen bring in their catch, quickly kill and clean the fish, and load them onto a truck headed for Chicago, some two hundred miles away. "They'll be served this evening in Chicago's finest restaurants," my mother marveled. Chicago!

When I came home from college for weekend visits and wanted to create distance between myself and a place once called Turd Town, rather than eating my mother's fried catfish, I baked or poached mine, as if it were salmon or halibut—anything but a fish pulled from the old, dirty, and familiar Mississippi.

∽

Nature's wonder: a fish like a cat that sports gracefully sweeping, whiskerlike barbels around its mouth, that rests by day and prowls by night, that gets in brawls with other cats, that slips, felinelike, past obstacles in logjammed water.

My father ran basket traps on the stretch of river between Memorial Auditorium and the railroad bridge. A catfish was lured into one of his baskets by a smelly morsel broken off a cheese brick; wooden slats kept it from swimming back out. To anchor a basket, my father tied a cinderblock to it with about fifty feet of old telephone cord. He marked the locations of his baskets by tying them in his memory to something stable on shore—a dock, tree, or cabin—so he would know where to drag the hook from the boat to snag the baskets and haul them up, hopefully full of slapping, writhing catfish. If my father brought up empty baskets, it may have been because the fish found tastier fare elsewhere. But, too, the baskets may have been vandalized. "Not all folks on the river are honest," my mother says. But often, my dad brought home a mess of flatheads. With its mottled yellow-brown skin, bad underbite, flattened skull between its tiny eyes, and squared-off tail, the flathead was, to my eyes, the ugliest of the catfish.

If my father wanted channel catfish, he went south of town and approached the river from a beach owned by the electric company. There the river bottom was more gravelly than muddy and the water clearer—just the way channel cat like it. My maternal grandparents were also avid fishers, though they preferred ponds and lakes, where they caught perch and crappie. It was with them that I caught my first fish, a bluegill. But in later years, after my grandparents moved to Burlington from Keokuk, my grandfather walked down the hill from his Main Street apartment with his fishing pole and the bait balls that he made from cornmeal and limburger cheese, and he, too, angled for channel catfish. With its streamlined form, deeply forked and pointy-tipped tail, curved and rayed anal fin, and dark freckles on its silvery sides, it was the most beautiful of the catfish.

∽

A survey conducted in 1968 revealed that if there was to be a state fish, most Iowans favored the channel catfish, *Ictalurus punctatus.* The late George L. Marzeck Sr. of West Burlington, a former writer, photographer, and illustrator for *Midwest Outdoors, Field and Stream,* and *Fur, Fish and Game,* spent decades campaigning to get the channel cat officially declared the Iowa state fish. After all, Iowa has a state rock (the geode), a state tree (the oak), a state flower (the wild rose), and a state bird (the eastern goldfinch). Why not a state fish? Marzeck, who signed the lowercase letter *g* in his first name as a stylized fishhook with a small barb on the end, preferred the bass, but because of the catfish's abundance in Iowa's waterways and the desires of the majority, it was the channel catfish that he promoted for the position of honor. "I've had outdoor writers from all over the country tell me, 'I never go through Iowa without stopping for one of your delicious catfish dinners,'" Marzeck told Radio Iowa. "So I says, 'Hey, let's ballyhoo this thing and maybe bring in some more revenue from people passing through.'" Marzeck always said catfish is the tastiest fish you can poke a fork into. "I don't think there's a place in Iowa that serves food that doesn't have catfish on the menu. When you have a church social or any kind of a gathering, what do you serve? Catfish and hush puppies, and coleslaw, maybe."

A joint resolution seeking to designate the catfish as the state fish offered several other reasons why this would be the most logical choice for the position of honor. The catfish not only is native and abundant, but also is found in all ninety-nine Iowa counties and is, in the words of the resolution, "easily recognizable by its slender scale-less body, deeply forked tail, fleshy whiskers, and sharp spines." It's easily and cheaply caught, excellent table fare, the state's most consumed fish, lucrative (Iowa's catfishers spend about $400 million a year in the pursuit), and the most preferred fish among Iowa anglers, reaching trophy size above thirty pounds and providing pole-bending action.

Not all Iowans approved of the idea of making this species a state symbol. In February 2001, the *Burlington Hawk Eye* reported that Garry Thomas, a member of the Burlington City Council and a friend of mine in high school, contended that because the catfish eats dead things, it would damage the state's reputation if it were chosen as state fish. "We should not be portrayed as a scavenger state," Thomas said. "We should not be linked to a fish like this when we're trying to build our image up." Some feel that the bass, with its fierce strikes, its aerial leaps and twists, its top-of-the-food-chain diet, and the specialized equipment that people invest in to catch it, is a more glamorous piscine river dweller. But Marzeck believed that it's the catfish that represents the character of Iowans. "The channel catfish prefers clean, clear water," he pointed out, "but it's tough enough to put up with a lot of crap."

Legislation promoting the catfish was introduced in the Iowa House and Senate several times between 1972 and 2011. Each time it failed. My suspicion is that there are too many men and women in the statehouse who don't spend enough time sitting on a riverbank holding a fishing pole. Despite the defeats, Marzeck continued campaigning with gusto on behalf of the catfish, writing hundreds of letters to state and local officials and giving school presentations at his own expense. Marzeck had been part of a group of six promoting the catfish, but as the fight dragged on, he was the only one left. Even after Marzeck was diagnosed with cancer, he continued his crusade. In a letter to a state senator, Marzeck wrote that "three of my doctors believe my continuing determination to get the channel catfish named the official state fish of Iowa is helping me put on a pretty good battle against my third bout of cancer." Marzeck died September 17, 2006, at age eighty-two without seeing the channel cat receive its due. Though the Iowa Senate passed the proposal in 2008, the demands of other legislation kept the House from voting on it that session.

∞

In a logjam at the bottom of the river near Burlington lives a giant catfish. In the stories we told about the monster, we usually compared him (it was always a "him") to mammals (as big as a dog, sheep, or grizzly bear) or vehicles (as big as a Volkswagen or school bus). Many of the tales about this mossy-backed behemoth were stories of loss or near loss: the disappearance of dogs, pigs, and other domestic animals; broken or lost tackle, arms, and legs; and near drownings. In some stories, the titan fish threatened the lives of those who worked on the bridges. Close encounters with the lunker so spooked the workers that they turned white-headed overnight and found safer jobs away from the river—like on the assembly line at the nuclear-weapons plant west of town. "Maybe every river town has one of these," my mother mused about the giant catfish.

An article in the June 23, 1998, *Hawk Eye* gives the authority of the printed word to the legends. Gene Murray reports that some claim that "Old Moe" is a two to three hundred-pound flathead, though "the wide-eyed commercial fisherman with the huge hole in his trammel net swears to have had him up once and his head would weigh more than that." Murray tells of the time when two young men, one from Iowa, one from Illinois, were determined to pull Old Moe from the river. Since flatheads love carp minnows, the fishers kept "a couple of 25 pounders ... in the horse tank behind the barn." Since the challengers knew that their regular equipment wasn't worthy of the task at hand, they mail ordered a huge, stainless-steel shark hook with a chain leader. For the mainline, they used two hundred yards of one-thousand-pound-test nylon rappelling rope. "Fearing that no manageable rod would handle the legendary might of Moe," explains Murray, "our heroes opted for a direct connection to the hitch on a four wheel drive pick-up." A crowd gathered; people placed their bets; an announcer narrated the action. Old Moe was fierce. The truck threw sand and gravel into the air as the tires spun. Eventually, Old Moe broke loose and got away. But the pursuit wasn't for naught: the two fishers reeled in a sixty-pound lower jaw.

River people have long been captivated by rumors of leviathan catfish. Perhaps the first written account of a monster catfish was that of the fur trader and explorer Louis Jolliet, who, with Jacques Marquette, a Jesuit missionary, paddled down the Mississippi in 1673 in search of the fabled Northwest Passage to the Orient for the governor of New France. Just north of what is now Alton, Illinois, Jolliet recorded in his journal: "We met from time to time these monstrous fish which struck so violently against our canoes that we took them to be large trees, which threatened to upset us." In *Life on the Mississippi*, Mark Twain says that Indians had warned the two travelers that "the river contained a demon 'whose roar could be heard at a great distance, and who would engulf them in the abyss where he dwelt.'" Twain reports that he had himself seen a Mississippi catfish that weighed 250 pounds and was more than 6 feet long. "If Marquette's fish was the fellow to that one, he had a fair right to think the river's roaring demon was come."

In 1765, over four hundred miles upriver from where Marquette and Jolliet were frightened by monster catfish, Peter Pond, a soldier, fur trader, explorer, and mapmaker in the Old Northwest and the Upper Mississippi, and his crew caught giant catfish. "We put our Hoock and Lines into the Water and Leat them Ly all nite. In the Morning we Perseaved there was fish at the Hoocks," Pond noted in his journal. "They Came Heavey. At Length we hald one ashore that wade a Hundred and four Pounds—a Second that was One Hundred Wate—a third of Seventy-five Pounds." Pond asked his men how many of them it would take to eat the largest fish, the 104-pounder, with "a large flat Head Sixteen Inches Betwene the Eise." Twelve men skinned it, cut it up, boiled it "in large Coppers," and "Sawed it up." They ate the entire fish, and "Sum of them Drank of the Licker it was Boild in."

My parents' friend Sam catfishes at Lock and Dam No. 18, north of Burlington; the drainage ditch near Iowa Highway 99; the Port of Burlington, a former barge-loading station that is now a State of Iowa Welcome Center; and the beach owned by the electric company. It was at the last that her five-foot, six-inch sister-in-law caught a catfish as tall as she is. Sam's brother waded into the water and wrestled the fish to the bank. A big fish fry followed.

Like Old Moe, these catfish swim in the murky area between fact and legend. But now there are monster catfish whose sizes have been verified with newspaper photographs and documentation through the International Game Fish Association. On May 22, 2005, Tim Pruitt, a factory worker from Fosterburg, Illinois, near Alton, pulled a 124-pound blue catfish, 58 inches long and 44 inches around, from the Mississippi below the Melvin Price Lock and Dam. Pruitt and the fish struggled for more than half an hour. At one point the fish was actually dragging Pruitt's boat. In a widely published photograph, Pruitt, a burly guy, holds a catfish the size of a thirty-four-gallon garbage can across his chest and abdomen. The fish is rather porpoiselike, with its smooth, blue-gray skin, blunt, round nose, slightly humped back, and forked tail. Pruitt donated his catch to the Cabela's store in Kansas City, where it would have lived in a giant aquarium if it hadn't died en route. A fisheries biologist with the Illinois Department of Natural Resources estimated that Pruitt's catch was at least thirty years old. I suspect that this fish inspired river-town legends about a fish as big as an SUV, bridge workers who now drive trucks, and some old fisher who claims to possess a lower jawbone too heavy to lift without help.

∞

It was during the Flood of 2008 that I realized that stories of giant catfish are more than just fish stories. At five o'clock in the morning on June 17, the Mississippi tore a hole more than three hundred yards long in the levee on the Illinois side of the river across from Burlington. The river, carrying cornstalks and other debris, poured into the Gulfport bottoms, moving at about a foot and a half per second. The force of the water pushed the village hall five feet off its foundation. The fast water trapped a man and two dogs in their vehicle on Highway 34. They were rescued by helicopter. Larry Gapen, the Carthage Lake Drainage District pump plant operator, and his dog, Molly, were still at the pump station when the Mississippi burst through the levee. "They came inside and got me and said the levee broke," Gapen told the *Hawk Eye*. "I tried to go out to the road but the water was covering the road so fast there [was] only one way. I told everyone to go to the levee." From that vantage point, Gapen watched the river swallow his house. He left the area by boat.

From Mosquito Park on a bluff above the Mississippi, I saw the sprawling river; the Great River Bridge, which led not from land to land but from water to water; the tops of the trees lining what had been the river's eastern shore; and, instead of the usual village of Gulfport, Highway 34, and fields of corn and soybeans: a vast and sparkling lake. Seventy billion gallons of water covered twenty-eight thousand acres in Henderson County, Illinois. June 18, a levee broke at Meyer, a village of forty to fifty people near Quincy, Illinois, about seventy miles downriver. It was the eleventh levee to fail on the Mississippi since the flooding began.

Because a levee breach on one side of the river lessens the severity of the flooding on the other side, the breach at Gulfport saved Burlington (population 26,000); the breach at Meyer saved Canton, Missouri (population 2,550). Levee breaks at Winfield and Foley, Missouri, saved homes and fields in Illinois. The various upriver levee breaks eased the threat in the greater St. Louis area (population 2.8 million). Nonetheless, many river dwellers lost homes and businesses; crops were buried beneath several feet of sand and debris; the toxic water rose halfway up some grain bins; travelers and residents were stranded because of the bridge and highway closings. I had gone home to help sandbag, but with the bridges closed, I couldn't cross to the east side of the river, where help was most needed.

Gulfport still hasn't recovered. Six months after the flood, only two businesses, Sam's Speakeasy and the ADM grain elevator, had reopened. Most houses were so badly damaged that they had to be demolished. In April 2010, almost two years after the flood, only sixty of the two hundred or so people who lived in Gulfport at the time of the flood had returned. But those who have come back are optimistic. They've rebuilt the town hall, are refurbishing the park with grant money from the state, and are seeking $12 million in buyouts and from other sources so they can build the city hall, a fire department, and housing outside of the floodplain. Henderson County is working to rebuild the levee so that it can regain its one hundred-year certification through the Federal Emergency Management Agency's

National Flood Insurance Program. In April 2009, voters approved a plan to build a five hundred–year levee that will cost about $37 million.

As I surveyed the submerged towns, farms, highways, and riverfronts during the Flood of 2008, I realized what the monster catfish stories are really about. As a child, I had heard stories about how dangerous and frustrating the river was—not only its floods, but also its low water during droughts, shifts in its course that reworked state and property lines, and its undertows that could pull you under and hold you there, which is why sane people don't swim in the river. But these stories harkened back to earlier times, prior to the 1930s and 1940s, when the U.S. Army Corps of Engineers tamed my stretch of the Mississippi, turning the once free-flowing river into a tightly controlled navigation system, thus providing what the natural river could not: a reliable nine-foot navigational channel to accommodate barge traffic. Now the greatest danger of entering the water isn't the undertow but the chemicals and wastes that it carries and the five hundred–year floods, those roaring and engulfing demons that are increasing in number and severity as the climate changes. To tell and retell stories about the monster catfish that you or someone else glimpsed or almost caught is a way of giving the river's dangers, mystery, beauty, bounty, and persistence form and substance, and so of making the river more manageable. To catch a catfish, even if it's too small to keep, is to momentarily master the river.

∞

I now live 320 miles west of the Mississippi, in Lincoln, Nebraska. The catfish in my freezer weren't pulled from the Mississippi by my parents or grandparents or brothers, but from lakes in southeastern Nebraska by my son, Ian. Instead of walking a few blocks to reach the Mississippi, I now have to drive over twenty miles just to see a water flow large enough to be called a river. If I want to see a river deep enough to float a barge, I have to drive over fifty miles.

Though I no longer live at Catfish Bend, several times a week I read in the online edition of my hometown newspaper about the river stages, the area fishing reports, the losses of buildings, people, and places that I used to know, and the city's continued movement westward, away from the river. Once or twice a year, I return to Burlington and other Mississippi River towns to do library or archival research about my stretch of the river and to take long riverside strolls. Often, I daydream of owning a rustic little cabin on stilts on the river side of the levee and have, on a couple of occasions, looked at riverfront property. While I'm no longer part of the daily life at Catfish Bend, because I spent my childhood there, a time when every experience was new and memorable and weighted with significance, a time when everything I knew about the river came to me through the stories of those inhabitants who had a long-lived intimacy with the place, I know the geography and the human response to it with a depth of love and understanding that I have yet to acquire in my "new" home of twenty years.

In the twenty-some years since I left Catfish Bend, I've acquired the formal knowledge that contextualizes the place I came from. The United States maps that hang in my university and home offices show the entire length of the Mississippi, from Lake Itasca to the Gulf of Mexico, which reminds me where my river comes from and where it goes after it flows past my hometown. When I look at the map, I remember Mississippi River sites that I've explored: the pre-Columbian burial and ceremonial mounds lining the river; the locks and dams; the great cities that prospered because of their proximity to the river; the little towns lost to floods; the wildlife refuges where waterfowl gather; the sites of former fur-trading posts and utopias and mussel-shell ("pearl") button factories; the condominiums, casinos, and shopping malls built perhaps in defiance, perhaps from collective amnesia on the floodplains. Now, when I look at the Upper Mississippi on the map, I remember the points where other rivers—the St. Croix, Yellow, Wisconsin, Rock, Iowa, Skunk, Des Moines, Illinois, Missouri, and Ohio—flow into mine. After these travels over the map, my eyes always come home to rest on the lower-lip-like bend in the river.

Catfish Bend was twice blessed. As Alfred T. Andreas noted in his 1875 *Andreas Illustrated Historical Atlas of the State of Iowa*, the alluvial and prairie soils of Des Moines County made it "one of the best agricultural counties in the state." And just outside our front door was a major transportation corridor that connected the Twin Cities to Burlington to St. Louis to Memphis to

New Orleans. In 1868, the Chicago, Burlington, and Quincy Railroad (the CB&Q) entered Burlington when it built a single-track railroad bridge over the Mississippi and established a repair shop, where both my grandfather and father would earn their bread and butter. In August 1872, 147 steamboats passed beneath the Burlington Railroad Bridge. A few decades earlier, flatboats and keelboats weighted with cargo created traffic jams on the river. Now, tows take their time moving petroleum, grain, coal, ammonia, and scrap metal up and down the river; passenger and freight trains pass through Catfish Bend several times a day.

During the latter half of the nineteenth century, Burlington became a booming industrial town, packing pork and milling grain and lumber. The 1911 *Encyclopedia Britannica* reports that in the early twentieth century, my hometown turned local and imported materials into "lumber, furniture, baskets, pearl buttons, cars, carriages and wagons, Corliss engines, waterworks pumps, metallic burial cases, desks, boxes, crackers, flour, pickles and beer." For several decades, Burlington was one of the premier lumber towns on the Upper Mississippi. Several local people prospered as furniture manufacturers, turning huge log rafts from Minnesota and Wisconsin into desks and cabinets and bureaus. In 1871, lumber shipping peaked, the beginning of the end for that industry. A headline in the November 29, 1897, *New York Times* warned, "Western Forests Doomed: Minnesota, Wisconsin, and Northern Michigan Will Soon Be

Depleted of Their Timber." In 1915, the last lumber raft stopped at Burlington. Ironically, the Leopold family, who lived on a high bluff above the river and who made a fortune crafting elegant desks, sideboards, and bookcases at the Leopold Desk Company with wood harvested from northern forests, brought forth a child who became one of the world's greatest ecologists and ethicists. In "The Land Ethic," an essay in his book *A Sand County Almanac and Sketches Here and There,* Aldo Leopold calls for a new conception of history. Instead of presenting the past only in terms of human enterprise, instead of merely recounting the wars and industries, the booms and busts, he directs us to understand historical events as "biotic interactions" between the people and the land, with the human as but one member of the "biotic team." Because "the characteristics of the land determine the facts quite as potently as the characteristics of the men who lived on it," Leopold contends, history, properly told, is the story of how people, successfully or unsuccessfully, interacted with the water, weather, soils, fish, plants, and other living creatures.

Stories about catfish and catfishers are one piece of the ecological history of my hometown. So, too, are stories about floods and our response to them. People have long been drawn to the Mississippi because of what it provides: catfish, mussels, waterfowl, water, wood, and energy. But living too close to the river poses dangers. It wasn't until quite recently in the history of human interactions with the Mississippi that people attempted to control it by dredging, straightening, damming, and leveeing. Many continue to see this as the answer to the river's cyclical flooding. Don Kerr, a Warsaw, Illinois, farmer, has drawn local support for his efforts to persuade the government to build a five hundred-year levee along the Upper Mississippi. According to Kerr's calculations, the known losses from the Flood of 2008 to farmers in Hancock and Adams counties in Illinois came to about $80 million, a total that he says doesn't yet include the cost of "about a half-dozen more unknown damages like stress and delayed purchases." Kerr figures that it will cost the government $40 million to raise the levee in his part of the river. A bargain, in Kerr's mind. So, too, for Mark Ford, a commissioner with the Henderson County Drainage District No. 2. In March 2009, Ford told the *Hawk Eye*, "If we can get the levees built up to the five hundred-year elevation, maybe there can be some more development in that bottom ground"—bottomland that recently was under water, debris, and toxic wastes. Because a study done by the U.S. Army Corps of Engineers shows that the cost benefits of the levee don't meet the Corps' one-to-one ratio requirement (i.e., for every dollar spent on levee improvements, there must be at least one dollar's worth of property protected), the plan to raise a five hundred–year levee in western Illinois hasn't received congressional support.

Tall levees offer a false sense of security that encourages risky development in flood-prone areas.

When levees fail, as they did at Gulfport, Meyer, Winfield, Foley, and other towns during the Flood of 2008 and at New Orleans during Hurricane Katrina, they do so spectacularly and sometimes catastrophically. Fortunately, a growing number of scientists and public policy makers now see levees as more of a problem than a solution, since they make the river run higher and faster. Wiser land use policies, which limit development near the river, and restoration of the great natural sponges that once lined the river (Iowa, Illinois, and Missouri have allowed over 80 percent of their wetlands to be lost to agriculture or development, making those states the national leaders in the destruction of wetlands) will do far more to minimize the damage from flooding than higher levees. So, too, will limiting the amount of fossil fuels that we burn. The carbon dioxide emitted into the atmosphere by the burning of oil, coal, and natural gas warms the air. Warmer air holds more water vapor than cooler air, which results in heavier, more intense rainfall events. This in turn causes the rivers to flood.

Some cities and larger towns along the Mississippi have been moving away from the river for several decades, though more for economic than environmental reasons. When I was in college during the late 1970s and early 1980s, the factories that had provided so many workers in my hometown with a good living and the money to send their children to college started leaving Burlington for the same reasons they left other midwestern cities and towns. A new mall pulled businesses and eventually the medical center away from what had once been the city's lifeblood: the river. Burlington began a long, slow decline that continues to this day, though the casino, the big-box retailers, and the medical center on the west side of town seem to be holding their own. Even though it's been many years since you could buy a new shirt, get a prescription filled, or watch a movie in downtown Burlington, the people of my hometown will never abandon the riverfront. One of the constants is that there will always be people who want to catch and eat catfish and tell stories about the big one they caught or that got away or that lives at the bottom of the river, too tough and wily to be caught by any of us.

It's been a long time since I've eaten catfish or any other animal flesh. But if I ever fall off the wagon and revert to my old ways, I know what form the indulgence will take. I won't dip the channel catfish in cornmeal batter and fry it. Rather, I'll bake it, seasoned only with a dash of salt, so that nothing will interfere with the flavor of the old, dirty, familiar, magnificent, and uncontrollable Mississippi River.

UPO WETLANDS TO DOYO ISLET

Louise Duff

I'm standing at the Ami Mountain Observatory in Busan, South Korea, surrounded by conservationists. We're looking down across the broad bay of the Nakdong River Estuary, flat sand-islands in the foreground, mountains in the distance. The sun is setting into a bed of haze on the horizon, gilding the sea with gleaming sheets of gold.

We've come for an outdoor performance to mark the end of a three-day meeting between the Korean Wetlands Network, Ramsar Network Japan and the World Wetlands Network, of which I'm the Chair. All of us have a deep affinity with water in the landscape—flowing rivers, quiet swamps, tide-washed estuaries. We work in wetland conservation aligned to the international Ramsar Convention on Wetlands.

The singer, Ildon Yang, stands before us dressed in traditional long robes, his black lacquered drum cradled in a wooden frame. His accompanist, Donghee Lee, is young and slim, with a sad, soulful face, long hair knotted in a loose bun, wearing the black T-shirt and baggy black pants of an urban artist.

Ildon bows deeply then stands to address his audience. His face lights up as he welcomes us in animated Korean before bursting into song—a tremulous, ancient chant that sounds like the earth itself. He beats his drum in a steady rhythm while Donghee bends over his classical contrabass, bowing the strings, first holding a single note then throbbing out a low melody that sings of the Nakdong river below.

The Nakdong is the longest river in South Korea, home to 13 million people. Once a free-flowing river teeming with fish, the Nakdong was "refurbished" with a series of eight dams as part of the controversial Four Rivers Project. The Four Rivers Project was the brain-child of conservative President Lee Myung-bak, formerly CEO of Hyundai Engineering and Construction. Engaging all four major construction companies in South Korea and spending around US$2 billion, Myung-Bak's government built 16 dams from 2009-11 on the Han, Geum, Yeongsan and Nakdong Rivers. Hundreds of kilometers of river were dredged, their banks cut-and-filled, serpentine bends straightened into channels, their riparian forests alive with birdsong paved over by concrete.

To justify the project, the government argued that it would meet five grand objectives. It would prevent floods, secure water supply, improve water quality, restore river ecosystems, create recreational areas and contribute to economic revitalization. Instead, ecosystem health and water quality crashed on all four rivers. The Nakdong was the worst afflicted.

Three days ago on World Rivers Day 2017, our gathering of conservation groups and civil society toured the river. We were led by local activists who campaigned against the Four Rivers Project and continue to call for its restoration. My own journey roamed wider, exploring nearby wetlands in the Nakdong catchment.

Today's haunting performance, gazing across the wounded estuary stretching towards the sunset, is a chance to reflect on this river and its people. It's a story of change brought by the flow of water, passion, politics and time. Destruction and conservation, restoration and hope.

Upo Wetlands

My exploration begins when Ms. Mikyung Moon picks me up at 9.30 am, five days earlier. She's warm, smart and speaks perfect English. We're on our way to Upo Wetlands, a Ramsar-listed wetland and education centre an hour away in Changyeong. Driving out of Gimhae, the freeways and white apartment blocks that bristle skyward like giant termite nests give way to backroads following the valley floor. We pass market gardens, rice paddies, orchards and forested hills.

Mikyung chats easily as we drive: "When I was young I grew up in the country. We were always in nature, in the forest, climbing down the mountains, playing in the caves. It taught me to be brave and face a challenge. My friends who grew up in the city are shy. They say, *I can't do it.* I'm always looking for the next adventure."

Returning to Korea after study in Sydney and work in Indonesia, Mikyung managed a wetland conservation project for the United Nations Development Program, and later worked for the Changwon Municipal Government. She was one of a group of local conservationists who mobilized to bring the tenth Ramsar Conference of Parties to Changwon in 2008. At the conference, Mikyung helped initiate the World Wetlands Network (WWN), supporting conservation and civil society groups to participate effectively and stay in contact. Now here I am ten years later, Chair of WWN, working with the same people to prepare for the 13th Ramsar wetlands meeting in Dubai. It's really something to circle back in history and meet the folks who started the Network. We're all honoured to meet each other—good vibes all round.

Arriving at Upo Wetlands Centre we share a meal at a small restaurant: a soup of teeny garden snails and endemic greens, dressed in lime, chilli and ginger. Food miles: zero. Mikyung knows a group of scientists at the next table, here to monitor waterbirds. They're excited the wetlands are hosting a family of Pheasant-tailed

Jacanas. These striking, endangered waders have been migrating here to breed for only the past three-years, perhaps due to climate change. Maybe we'll see them!

Our guide at the Upo Wetlands is Mr. Insik Lee, a retired school teacher. He is a good-looking man with silver hair, a warm smile, twinkling eyes and a beautiful presence. He's known as the father of wetland conservation, planting the seed for the Ramsar conference and inspiring many teachers to become custodians of the catchment.

Mr Lee had a vision to conserve Upo Wetlands in 1991, and started campaigning. The wetlands were declared a Ramsar site of international importance in 1998, and are now managed for conservation and wise-use. The core zone is fully protected, while the buffer zones allow for local livelihoods such as farming and ecotourism. Mr Lee promised the local community that after he retired he would live here and help look after Upo. And now here he is, guardian of the wetlands, tour guide extraordinaire.

Walking along the levy bank, we see 100 or so Common Teal that arrived last week from Siberia. Spotted-bill Ducks are dabbling in the shallows. Elegant Greater Egrets and Grey Herons stalk the water's edge hunting for prey. An Azure Kingfisher flashes past and pounces on a skink, expertly smacking it against a rock before eating it. Missing now in early Autumn are the thousands of Bean Geese and Baikal Swans that migrate here every winter.

Mr Lee explains that Upo is one of four connected wetlands that make up a circular basin 24km in perimeter. The wetlands are surrounded by forested mountains and 12 small rural villages ("*These villages: [have only] old man, old woman. No young people*"). A levy bank separates the wetlands from rice paddies. The natural flow of water through the wetlands has been interrupted by the levy bank and one of the dams constructed upstream on the Nakdong River for the Four Rivers Project. Still, the wetlands are a valuable refuge for waterbirds and people.

We come upon a sheltered bay where the surface of the water is almost completely covered in vivid green waterlilies with giant leaves like floating wheels one-metre across. They reflect the sun like a shining mirror. The sight is dazzling—as if the lake is paved with brilliant silver. Strange thorns cover the leaves, stems and sheaths of the deep purple flowers emerging from the depths then opening to face the sun. Prickly-leaved Water Lilies are an endangered lotus which fertilize their own buds underwater. These are flowering for the first time in four-years. How fortunate we are to see them!

And there, delicately picking their way across the lily-pads, are Pheasant-tailed Jacanas; a father and his three babies. Looking through binoculars I see the handsome male's striking black and white plumage, his long, pheasant-like tail and gold feathers on the nape of his neck. The babies are cute fluff-balls with long, skinny legs and enormous feet. Watching them is extraordinary, silhouetted against the dazzling light, hunting for waterbugs.

Pheasant-tailed Jacana females are polyandrous, mating with multiple partners. She sits on the eggs, only venturing away for short periods to feed. Once the hatchlings are born responsibility passes to the male, who shepherds them closely. A Kestrel flies overhead and we watch the father gather up the babies under his wings, only their skinny feet poking out. He retreats to hide in the reedbed.

The whole scene is astonishing! I feel enraptured in the glorious beauty of nature. It's difficult to tear ourselves away and return on the busy freeway to my love-hotel in the red-light district of Gimhae.

Nakdong River – Haman Weir

The next day, our formal tour of the Nakdong River begins. Our first stop is Haman Weir, one of eight dams built on the Nakdong River for the Four Rivers Project. We pile out of the bus and walk along the top of the huge dam wall, stretching 500 metres from one bank to the other. It's just one component of a massive engineering project that altered 13 km of the Nakdong by dredging the bottom, clearing natural vegetation, re-shaping and formalizing the banks and adding scour protection and a water pumping and distribution system.

We stop half-way along the dam wall, where Ms. HeeJa Im, a Policy Director with the Korean Federation for Environmental Movement informs us about the

Four Rivers Project and its impacts. Haman Weir and the other seven structures are having a devastating effect on ecosystem health. The obstruction to water flow causes stagnation and stratification of the water column: without sufficient current, the surface water is warmed by the sun and traps cold-water at the bottom. Dissolved oxygen falls and eutrophication affects the river for tens of kilometres. Every summer, toxic blue-green cyanobacteria algae outbreaks paint the water fluorescent green, rendering the river unsuitable for swimming and stock-water. Dredging and channelization increases water velocity and erosion during floods. Commercial species of fish and eels are unable to swim upriver to spawn, collapsing fisheries and threatening livelihoods. Water upstream is maintained at 6m. As a result, groundwater is rising, impacting on production of rice paddies. The vulnerable White-naped Crane, once a beloved annual visitor from Mongolia that visited to over-winter on the Nakdong, has lost its habitat on the river's edge. This same sad story has been repeated throughout the Four Rivers Project.

Civil society organisations campaigned against the Four Rivers Project, and continue to call for restoration of the Nakdong River. The current President Mr. Moon Jae-in from the Democratic Party of Korea made an election commitment to reverse the Four Rivers Project and restore the Nakdong River. He was elected in May 2017. The municipal government of Busan has also committed to restoring the river. Both levels of government are navigating a policy shift from managing water for flood and disaster mitigation to managing for drinking water and ecological health.

There are complex social, economic and environmental issues to work through with a range of stakeholders and competing interests. Efforts are underway but it will be a slow process. A restructure of the ministries will bring river management under the Department of Environment, led by a Minister who actively campaigned against the Four Rivers project. Environmental modelling is underway, and there's a program of community consultation to negotiate a path through the conflicting views between water users and environmental groups. The Minister maintains a high level of communication with the conservation and civil society sectors, who are monitoring and supporting the process to ensure the restoration project proceeds as promised. There is great hope that the ecological health of the river will be restored.

Hwapocheon Wetland

Downstream I visit Hwapocheon Wetlands with Mikyung Moon. Hwapocheon Wetlands is a back-swamp of the Nakdong River covering three square kilometers, with an Ecological Centre that educates the local community, visitors and school children. Hwapo is near Bongha Village, the birth place of former Democratic Party President Roh Moo-hyun, who declared the region as an organic farming district to promote the value of chemical-free rice paddies for biodiversity.

We wander around the wetlands on a visitor trail edged by a scramble of vegetation: pretty pink-flowering Persicaria; native honeysuckle with orange and cream flowers that can be infused into a tea to treat asthma; and small yellow flowers used to make a brilliant saffron dye. Water chestnuts grow at the water's edge and a flock of tiny, lightning-quick Vinnous-throated Parrotbills flit through reeds. In the trees there are huge, untidy magpie nests. A pair of common Kestrels soar overhead. We come upon a small temple, its roof thatched with reeds. A banner strung between the trees reminds visitors that *"concern for roadkill of amphibians presents the ultimate respect for life."*

Back near the Visitors Centre, we see an artificial nest atop a tall pole. It was built in the hope it would be used by a rare and much-loved Oriental White Stork that visited annually for three years from 2014. The Stork was a tagged female named Bongha, born as a result of a breed-and-release program in Toyoka Japan in 2012. She has shunned the nest, instead building her own in a transmission tower, causing concern for the villagers.

Oriental Storks are a large white stork with a flash of scarlet skin left bare around the eyes. They nest on tall trees and artificial structures, and feed on fish and small animals. Their preferred habitat is freshwater wetlands and rice paddies, but they're also occasionally found on tidal flats. This Stork is listed as endangered, because it has suffered a rapid decline due to deforestation, wetland reclamation, agricultural chemical pollution, overfishing, and disturbance. Bongha didn't come this year, and the villagers worry for her welfare. I hope she returns.

After our walk we visit a local restaurant, leaving our shoes at the door and joining workmen on their lunch break, dining at long low tables. We eat catfish soup, a local specialty flavoured with fermented red peppers. Mikyung dips a raw green chilli into white miso paste. There is refreshing green tea and an acorn pudding.

Nakdong Estuary Ecological Centre

At the bottom of the Nakdong River lies the Nakdong Estuary Eco Centre. Mr. SungBae Park, head of the education program has kindly offered to take me and my colleague Dr. Jacky Judas birdwatching on Doyo Islet. This is not just any birding expedition. Our mission is to spot the incredibly rare Spoonbill Sandpiper.

According to the East Asian Australasian Flyway Partnership, this little shorebird is one of the most threatened birds on the planet. Each year it breeds in the Russian Far East, migrates through Russia, Japan, North Korea, South Korea and China to winter in southern China, Bangladesh, Myanmar and Thailand, 8,000km from its breeding grounds. The species declined from an estimated 2,000-2,800 breeding pairs in the 1970s to 1,000 pairs in 2000 to less than 250 pairs in 2014.

Our Korean host, Mr. Kuncheol Kim has been monitoring Spoonbill Sandpipers here in Busan for the past few years. His sightings have fallen from an average of ten per year, to three this year. Just last week a solitary bird was seen on Doyo Island. We're in with a chance!

We pile into a zodiac inflatable with a tiny 15 HP outboard and motor 40 minutes across the shallow bay to Doyo-dong (islet). Once there, we cruise along the shore observing a big mixed flock of Eurasian and Far Eastern Curlew. Their distinctive calls drift on the breeze. Curlew are the biggest shorebird and also one of the quickest to take flight when disturbed. Being in the boat skimming past with our quiet little motor they barely notice us. We get a good look—the Eurasians with pale rumps, the Far Eastern a darker brown. I'm surprised how fast they run!

We cruise to another spot and see a flock of Pacific Golden Plover, Terek Sandpiper, a lone Bar-tailed Godwit, and Spotted Greenshank. Where there's shorebirds, there's predators. A Black Kite perches on a log nearby and an Osprey sits on a fishing pole. We search the flock for Spoonbill Sandpiper. I look high. I look low. I look in the centre of the flock, I look on the edge. I look for outliers. No luck.

Once ashore I'm surprised to see footprints of Chinese Water Deer and Racoon Dog. There's loads of fishing rubbish—floats, buoys, nets and traps. The beach is strewn with large white cockle shells, some as big as my hand. Red Ghost Crabs side-step back and forth, excavating their homes and scooping up food.

There is a large flock of Lesser Sand Plovers, some juveniles running and hunting. A group of five Dunlin sit in a depression in the sand with their backs to us. Spoonbill Sandpiper? No. We walk along the beach and Jacky sets up his scope, training it on a large mixed flock with hundreds of shorebirds. There are 200 or so Red-necked Stint. SungBae says they counted over 1000 last week. Jacky is an expert birder, showing us Sanderlings, Ruddy Turnstones, and about 50 Kentish Plovers amongst the Lesser Sand Plovers. He shows me how to spot them, with their smaller bill and broken banding on the collar.

Excitement! A Peregrine Falcon soars in like a bullet, putting up the whole flock. They wheel and spin to evade the predator. The flock fly as one, flashing past us. It's an incredible site! Then, even better, they land in front of us, right on the watermark. A Hobby joins the hunt and they take to the sky again. We watch the breathtaking sight until they settle again, further down the beach.

We see a pair of Broad-billed Sandpiper with a distinctive black band on top of their heads and double streaks at the eye. The Pacific Golden Plovers are in golden breeding colours, much different to the plumage I'm used to seeing in Australia. They look big against the Sandpipers. I watch one with a juicy dragonfly in its beak, which it smacks against the ground a couple of times, then eats.

The sea breeze comes in and the waves pick up. SungBae says we'd better go. Intensely, we scan the beach for that elusive, rare, lonely Spoonbill Sandpiper. It could be here, right now! But we don't find it. Nevertheless, it has been a wonderful day of birding. We walk back across the island and push off in the Zodiac. Motoring back across the bay the Osprey flies right above us and pauses as if to show us the fish he's holding in his talons. The Osprey launches itself from its post and flies off down the coast. The sea is teeming with silver fish leaping out of the water and flashing in the sun. SungBae comments "they say catch me if you can. Sometimes they jump into the boat!"

Journeys End

Looking towards the mainland, we can see the massive Estuary Dam, the last of the Four Rivers Project structures. It prevents the mixing of salt and freshwater, essential to estuarine ecosystem health. With so much development in South Korea, it's heartening that conservation and civil society groups are campaigning to conserve nature. Undoing the Four Rivers Project and restoring the Nakdong River will be complex, with competing interests and a range of environmental, social and economic issues to be considered. Conservationists are working with the government and maintaining pressure to ensure this valuable river and its estuary are restored for shorebirds, fish and the community

It's six years since the World Wetlands Network drew international attention to the Four Rivers Project at the 11th Ramsar wetland meeting in Romania. Issuing the project with a Grey Globe Award for wetlands under threat; we highlighted the government's failure to undertake proper environmental evaluation, allowing the long-term value of the river and its wetlands to be destroyed.

And ten-years has passed since the 10th Ramsar wetland meeting in Changwon. The conservation and civil society leaders who instigated the meeting and the World Wetland Network are still working at the front-line of wetland conservation and education, with an ambitious program planned to celebrate a decade of action. It was wonderful for us all to meet, restore ourselves in nature, strengthen our relationships and renew our commitment to wetland conservation.

TEMPERATE FLOODPLAIN RIVERS

Temperate Floodplain River ecoregions are dominated by a single mid-latitude large river system, with a cyclically flooded, fringing floodplain. This ecoregion may also contain wetland complexes composed of internal deltas, marshes, or swamps, associated with the main river system.

THREE WATER STORIES

Anthony Birch

A freeway story

I turned thirteen in 1970. My large family were living in a crumbling terrace in a lost triangle of Collingwood, and inner suburb of Melbourne. Our family were hemmed in by the Collingwood football ground, a railway-line and goods yards, and a row of derelict nineteenth century textile mills. Behind the vacant factories lay a treasure; the Birrarung (Yarra) River, Dights Falls and another site of dereliction, the Deep Rock Basin, a swimming club built on a bank of the river sixty years earlier, which had become a ruin. This section of the river would occupy my teenage years, and would provide the source of my 2015 novel, *Ghost River*.

A dominant theme of both the novel and my teenage memory of that time is the terrible level of neglect and vandalism the river suffered. For over a hundred years the Birrarung had been treated as little more than an open sewer for the noxious industries built along its western bank. The river was also the dumping ground for the unwanted; stolen cars, animal carcasses, and those who occasionally suicided, by jumping from one of the many bridges spanning the river, with their suit pockets weighed down with stones. With Melbourne competing with Sydney as the 'gangland capital of Australia' throughout the twentieth century, the river was sometimes the last resting place of members of Melbourne's criminal underground.

In 1971, the Victorian state government came up with the idea to build a new freeway, beginning outside my front gate, stretching into the leafy eastern suburbs. It was a plan that would destroy country. The freeway, planned to abut *my* river, would consist of five lanes in each direction, a utopian solution that would put an end to one of Melbourne's most congested traffic locations. Or so claimed the glossy brochures dropped in the letterboxes of homes that would be demolished to turn a dream into reality. It would be only a short time after the opening of the Eastern Freeway that the state's most recent super artery, opened to allow the city to breathe, would clog the city's veins yet again. Over the following forty years, many more freeways and extensions have been built, crisscrossing and extending the infamous Melbourne sprawl; a city that has undergone more than one quadruple by-pass which is yet to save the patient.

The building of the Eastern Freeway required the obliteration of a vital section of the river, at its confluence with the Merri Creek, a once majestical waterway, winding its way into the north across Wurundjeri land. The Merri, as equally neglected as the Birrarung, faces a daily battle against urbanisation, in the form of household rubbish, chemical waste and weed infestation. If our river and creek valleys are 'the lungs of the city', historically, we have force-fed them toxins.

To visit the confluence today is to engage in a fiction. An interpretive sign where the two waterways meet instructs visitors that it was this *very* site where the first 'Aboriginal school' was erected, to educate local Indigenous children who had become the subjects of the colonial project. It may seem a harmless story to tell. And yet, it reflects the omissions of both narrative and landscape histories underpinning the colonisation. Firstly, as with many ventures that set out to 'civilise the native', the Merri Creek school was a failure. Attendance was fleeting, if non-existent, and Aboriginal communities of the area and its surrounds quickly lost faith in the empty promises of colonial authorities, that their customary way of life would be retained and *protected*.

The 'site' of the school's location is not the site of the school at all. It cannot be so, as when the freeway was being built a section of the river was destroyed by bulldozers and explosives. (The regular blasts would rattle my nearby bedroom window). The original meeting of river and creek was around a hundred metres north, and the location that people visit today is an ornamental construction with an ecological and human history less than fifty years old.

Such fibbing may not seem major when measured against the 'big lies' of colonial history, such as the widespread murder of Indigenous people across Australia, and the ecological destruction of country. After all, what's a mere hundred metres of lost or fictionalised country? Well, it's everything. It's the basis of another form of *denialism*, within Australia and western-colonial societies across the globe; the denialism of colonial violence, of attempted dispossession, the disregard shown for the rights and autonomy of country, and of course, the denial of climate change and the urgent need to work for climate justice. When we tell stories of place fiction can play a key role. But we must identify it as such, rather than use it as a convenient mask.

An upriver story

When I was around fourteen a friend and I stole a bicycle from the Victoria Park railway station. We spent the next hour or so rattling around the cobblestoned back streets of Collingwood, me being dinked on the handlebars. We eventually became bored. (I also had a sore arse). We bought a meat-pie each for lunch, rode the bike down to the river and sat above Dights Falls eating the pies and smoking cigarettes. It was then that my friend told me he'd once walked upriver for a day with one of his uncles, who made his living from breeding ferrets and catching rabbits.

During the walk, they visited water holes and ponds, none of which ran into the river itself, or appeared on any map. He also told me there were eucalypt trees in the water holes that 'old blackfellas' had used to make bark canoes, scar trees. Without another word between us we hopped on the bike, my friend peddling furiously along a narrow track. We rode for miles in the rain, by a massive paper-mill spewing smoke from chimneys, by the towers of a nineteenth-century 'lunatic' asylum, occasionally getting bogged in near-swamp conditions. I would have to jump off the handlebars and walk on until we came to firmer ground.

Just as I was losing faith in the truth of my friend's story, he turned off the track. We parked the bike against a tree and I followed my friend through the thickest stand of trees that a boy who had rarely travelled two miles out of the centre of the city had seen. I trailed him through the bush, my thin running shoes buried in mud. The trees above us thickened and it became dark. I could hear the call of many birds, a foreign but comforting sound. Further on, the landscape gradually thinned and I could see the sky above me. The trail ended suddenly and I was surprised to find myself standing before a still stretch of water, stained with what I now know to be the tannins of bark and fallen eucalypt leaves.

We sat on the bank and smoked more cigarettes. Except for the birdsong there was no sound in the air, a sensation I had never experienced before. I watched a water bird gracefully glide across the surface of the water, also without making a sound. When I think back to that first visit to the billabong what I remember most clearly was that, although I had no words for how I felt, no poetry with which to express myself, it was the first time in the life of an Aboriginal 'slum kid' that country had spoken to me. Although I wasn't looking forward to the long and bumpy ride home in the rain, it was not the reason for me wanting to stay by the water. Without understanding why, I had never felt so at ease with myself.

That night, we arrived at my back gate after dark. I knew I would be in trouble from my dad, but I didn't care. Before leaving him, I wanted to say something about the day's adventure to my friend. I do remember that I thanked him for showing me his secret place, but also knew it wasn't enough. Lying in bed that night and thinking about the billabong, I realised that I wanted to say to my friend that it was a *beautiful* place, but couldn't do it. Which one of us would have been more embarrassed by the word, I couldn't say. After all, at the time, we thought of ourselves the budding kings of a concrete jungle, and taking aside the romance of a life of thuggery, we lived in a world where violence was rarely threatened, but often practiced. If I forgot about the billabong for a time, I now believe that it came from having been denied the language to speak of it, to know it.

A billabong story

I live in Carlton, about a hundred metres away from the house I was born into sixty years ago. People who know me well, also know that distance running has guided my life for almost forty years now. It saved me from alcoholism at a young age, swore me away from cigarettes, and provided my mind with the clean slate I needed to discover a love of writing. I have run by many rivers in Australia; in Perth, Adelaide, Brisbane, and of course, my home town of Naarm (Melbourne). I have also run in cities around the world, including Wellington, Tokyo, Berlin, London, San Francisco, Gdansk and Banff. Most lifelong runners have a favourite run, a special route, where they feel 'at home' with themselves. I have such a run, one that returns me to the billabong.

I prepare for my run with a public transport 'swipe card' in the pocket of my running shorts and some coins for the telephone in case I do an injury, break down and need to call my wife. (This has never happened to me, but I have learned in life to prepare for all manner of potential disasters. And no, I have never had a mobile phone, which means I do not fully adhered to the notion of preparing for all disasters). I leave home and catch the nearby train, get out at Heidelberg station and begin the twelve- kilometre run home, most of the distance being along a trail skirting the Birrarung.

Most runners are also pendants, each possessing a minimum of at least one inexplicable idiosyncrasy. I have several, one of which used to be the cardinal rule, *never stop*; not for an injury, a pedestrian, road train or traffic light. In older age, I have gradually weaned myself off this suicidal commandment. The need to stop can actually beat chronic injury or death, I have decided. I didn't realise until I began my first river run from Heidelberg several years ago, that I would be more than happy to stop during a run and contemplatively *be* with country. It was on that first run that I became eerily familiar with surroundings that I thought I had not visited before. It was on that first run that as I was jogging by a stand of might eucalypts that I realised I had returned to the billabong.

It sits around the halfway point of my run, and is now surrounded by the imposition of 'civilisation' non-existent when I first visited the water. I approach the billabong from a hilltop. If it is a sunny morning its surface reflection will wink at me. If the wind is blowing from the south, I will pick up the scent of silted tea-stained water. The Eastern Freeway runs along the southern fringe of the billabong, and the flow of traffic is so constant that sitting by the water and listening, it is difficult to discern the sounds of an individual car or truck engine. The guttural hum is singular and unbroken. Remarkably, the birdcall remains clear. I'm not sure if it has something to do with a variance in pitch, but the birds seem to have little trouble singing above the traffic.

It is not possible to know where I sat on the afternoon I first visited the billabong over forty-five years ago. Memory is always suspect, and the landscape surrounding the billabong has changed dramatically over the years. The long section of riverbank running parallel to the freeway has been 'beautified', and the lush and private golf courses each side of the billabong compete with it for water. Most days when I visit, I sit and watch the passing joggers, dog walkers, cyclists and kite-flyers. I'm happy that they enjoy the river, and I hope they also care for it. But occasionally, I wish I could have it to myself. I wish I could enjoy the billabong in the way I did the day of our bike ride, knowing and not knowing how fortunate I was.

Selfishness is no virtue. What I wish for the billabong most of all, and my relationship to it, is that it continues to survive all it has been confronted by. Before the outsiders arrived in Wurundjeri country the billabong enjoyed a vital ecological connection with other waterways on country. Many of them have since been suffocated by occupation and development. The vast network of wetlands surrounding the Birrarung, from its birth in the mountains to its mouth at what we now call Port Phillip Bay, previous acted as both a repository of life and a sponge, absorbing distributing water across large tracts of land. These days the river is *governed*, held in place, against its will. The same could be said for the billabong. And yet, its beauty and tenacity remain a force.

THE WILLAMETTE

Kathleen Dean Moore

I wanted my daughter to lie in the tent, pressed between her brother and her father, breathing in the air that flows from the Willamette River at night, dense with the smell of wet willows and river algae. I wanted her to inhale the smoke of a driftwood fire in air too thick to carry any sound but the rushing of the river and the croak of a heron, startled to find itself so far from home. I wanted the chemical smell of the tent to mix with the breath of warm wet wool and flood through her mind, until the river ran in her veins and she could not help but come home again. That is why, on the weekend before my daughter left for Greece, I made sure that the family went river-camping on the Willamette.

∞

My daughter comes from a long line of people with strong homing instincts. My daughter's grandmother, my mother, was born in a river town, Thornaby-on-Tees, Yorkshire, in a brick house three blocks from the North Sea. Although she breathed the seaweed wind, she never walked on the beach below the limestone cliff at the end of her street. Warning signs and long coils of barbed wire protected the homeland against German invasion and kept my mother away from the sea.

Her father was one of the few men left at home in England during World War One. He was a ships' model builder who carved little wooden warships, patterns for the shipyards at Sunderland. Sometimes he brought his work home. My mother's strongest memory of England was the fragrance of fresh cedar curling under his plane and falling in long coils on the kitchen table. As he worked the wood, my grandfather sang Scottish folk songs—*You take the high road and I'll take the low road*—and the Navy hymn, *for those who perish on the sea.*

One night, my grandfather took my mother into the city to see where the zeppelins had firebombed the street car barns. Under cover of darkness, the zeppelins had moved slowly, silently, upriver to the shipyards, following the light of the ships on the Tees. They dropped their bombs, turned, and ran back to the sea. After that, blackout was imposed, and the zeppelins, when they returned, followed moonlight reflected on the river. My mother thought how beautiful the river must have appeared to the German airmen, its surface ablaze in reflected light from exploding buildings, and how anxious they must have been to get back home.

After the war, the shipyards shut down and my grandfather—unemployed and uneasy—began to think about emigrating. He argued for America because it was the only country that printed "In God We Trust" on its money. My grandmother refused to leave home unless she could come back to Thornaby-on-Tees every four years for the rest of her life. When my grandfather made her that promise, she gave away everything that wouldn't fit in three tea chests and dressed her children in their best clothes for the trip to America. Their destination was Cleveland, where an uncle had an extra room.

From the day they arrived, the family saved everything they had for four years and then, every four years, spent everything they had saved to go home. They traveled on the Cunard Line, second class. I have the picture postcards they sent back to America: yellowing photographs of oversized ships lined with tiny people wearing hats and waving. I also have ten teacups, one for every trip. They are decorated with painted ivy or pictures of the Queen. One says, *there'll always be an England.*

∞

When I was first married, we lived in an apartment above a delicatessen in Cleveland. The apartment had a balcony overlooking a major arterial. Evenings, we sat on the balcony in lawn chairs and watched the city life flow out of Cleveland in heavy white cars. One night we drove into the city to see the oil slicks burning on the

Cuyahoga River. We couldn't get close enough through the brickyards and factory gates to see the river. But we could see thick black clouds trapped in the rivercourse, glowing red underneath.

We began to think about leaving Cleveland. My husband argued for Oregon, because it had clean, cold rivers. So we moved to the Willamette Valley and made our home here. But I returned to Cleveland every year at Christmastime.

I have a picture in my memory of the drive through darkness to the Portland airport, with white fog flowing down the Willamette River as if even the air ran to the sea. I have a picture of the airport in early morning darkness. People are crowded together with their coats on, some sleeping curled up in chairs, their belongings in piles beside them. Everyone is solicitous, subdued, uneasy, as I imagine people to have been in the harshly-lit tunnels under London during the War.

Fewer and fewer things drew me back to Cleveland each year, but still I went. At first there was the house I grew up in, and my mother and my father and my two sisters, and the carols we always sang after supper. We sang slowly, in four-part harmony—deep, rich, thick Methodist chords. My mother chose the songs and gave us the pitch. *Winds through the Olive Trees, four verses.* And there were the English family foods—roast beef and Yorkshire pudding and decorated cookies between layers of wax paper in the roasting pan. We always took a picnic to the park in the snow, turning the picnic table on its side to shelter us from the wind coming off the lake. And always, there was the same joke about how the house was so full of people that we would have to cut off the back half of the Christmas tree and wedge it up against the wall.

But the house dropped out of the picture when my mother and father moved to a smaller place. My sisters got married and moved to bright new houses in the suburbs near Pittsburgh and Baltimore. Then my mother died. We couldn't pitch the songs. My father got sick. And so the rituals dropped away one by one, until there was nothing left at home except my father and the joke about half a Christmas tree. Finally, it seemed that the only reason to go home for Christmas was that someone needed to be there to hear my father tell the joke.

∞

I know a biologist who studies the homing instinct in garter snakes. He says that garter snakes spend the winters clustered together in rock piles underground, ancestral wintering dens that may have been home to the snakes for a thousand years. In the spring, all the snakes crawl out and travel, maybe half a mile. Each one establishes a home base for the summer, a pile of leaves or the space under a fallen log. They travel out each day, but each night they make their way back home along the same trails. When biologists draw a snake's wanderings on a map of the land, the lines are thick, drawn back and forth, back and forth, like rays extending out from a home base. In the fall, the adults travel back to spend the winter with their relatives in their ancient family home.

Before they return to the den, the females give birth to a pile of lithe little snakes and then move on, leaving the babies to fend for themselves. The babies spend the winter, who knows where. But the next fall, the yearlings travel back unerringly to the ancestral home—a place they have never been. As they go home, they will pass over other dens that would be perfectly good places to spend the winter, not stopping until they get to the den that shelters their own elderly aunts and distant relations.

Scientists know so much about homing in animals: Bees orient to polarized light. Salamanders steer by lines of geomagnetic force. Garter snakes follow scent. Pigeons use the position of the sun. Songbirds follow the stars. They are all drawn to a place proved to be safe by the hard, undeniable fact of their own existence.

But who has studied the essential issue? What will draw our own children back home?

∞

By the time we got all our camping gear stowed away in the driftboat, it was late afternoon. In the shadows of the riverside cottonwoods, the air was cold and sharp. So we drifted along the eastern bank of the river, glad for the warmth of the low light. We pulled up onto the gravel beach of an island thick with willows and set up the tent on a pocket of sand.

After supper, my daughter and I walked down the shore. We wore high black rubber boots and walked sometimes in, sometimes out of the water, the round rocks grinding and rolling under our feet. Far ahead, a beaver slapped its tail against the river. We talked quietly—about her visa, about loneliness, about how the skyline of the distant coast range seemed to glow in the dark.

Fog thickened the darkness, so even though it wasn't late, we turned back toward our supper fire. We didn't talk much on the way back, but we sang like we often do along the edge of a river, where the density of the air and the rush of the river make the music rich and satisfying. We sang the Irish Blessing—my daughter sang the soprano part—and we did fine, the river singing the bass line, the rocks crunching under our boots, until we got to the last blessing: May the rain fall softly on your fields. Then I couldn't do it anymore. I sent my daughter back to the fire alone. I lay face down on the round rocks and cried until the steam from my lungs steeped down into the dried mud and algae, and the hot breath of the river rose steaming and sweet around my face.

∞

Maybe the homing instinct is driven by traditions: hanging Christmas stockings each year on nails pushed into the same little holes in the mantel. Maybe it is driven by smells or tastes or sounds. But maybe the homing instinct is driven only by fear. On the road, at dusk and away from home, the foreboding, the oppression of undefined space, can be unbearable.

Pioneers knew this dread; they called it *Seeing the elephant.* Starting out, the wide open spaces were glorious—the opportunities, the promise, the prairie, all fused with light streaming down from towering clouds. Then suddenly the clouds became an elephant, a mastodon, and the openness turned ominous. The silence trumpeted and the clouds stampeded. Dread blackened the edges of the pioneers' vision. They saw the elephant and turned their wagons around, hurrying through the dusty ruts back to St. Louis. They had to go back. They had to get home.

The French existentialists knew that feeling: *la nausée*, existential dread. The pioneers—they, we—walk out into a world we think makes sense. We think we understand what things are and how they are related. We feel at home in the world. Suddenly, without warning, the meaning breaks off the surface, and the truth about the world is revealed: Nothing is essentially anything. The prairie gapes open—"flabby, disorganized mass without meaning," Sartre said. Pioneers can create meaning by their decisions, but those decision will be baseless, arbitrary, floating.

This discovery comes with a lurch, thick in your stomach, like the feeling you get when you miss a step on the stairs. When the feeling comes over you, you have to go home, knowing that home doesn't exist—not really, except as you have given meaning to a place by your own decisions and memories.

∞

Robins singing woke me up in the morning, a whole flock of robins at the edge of the Willamette. Each robin was turned full into the sun. I climbed out of the tent and sat cross-legged on the gravel, my face turned toward the warmth, my eyes closed, bathed in pink light. Soon my daughter, in long underwear and rubber boots, ducked out of the tent and walked into the river to wash her face. She scooped up a pot of river water and carried it to the kitchen log to boil for tea. Crossing to the campbox, she rummaged around inside until she found matches, scratched a match against a stone, lit the stove, and set the teapot on the burner. Then she sat on the broad log in a wash of sunlight, pulling her knees up to her chest and tilting her face toward the light. Her hair, in the sun, was as yellow as last winter's ash leaves in the windrows on the beach.

∞

Scientists say that a wasp can leave its hole in the ground, fly from fruit to fruit, zigging and zagging half the day, and then fly straight home. A biologist once moved the three rocks that framed a wasp's hole and arranged them in the exact same pattern, but in a different place. The wasp landed between the rocks, right were its hole should have been, and wandered around, stupefied.

My three rocks are the Willamette River. Whenever I walked out of the airport, coming home from a visit to my father's house, I could smell the river, sprayed through sprinklers watering the lawn by the parking lot. The willow-touched water would wash away the fumes of stale coffee and jet fuel and flood me with relief. This is what I want for my daughter.

RIVER OF THE PAST

Conor Mihell

The crack is sickening. One moment I'm lugging an 80-pound wood-canvas canoe across an overgrown backcountry portage, sidestepping through a jackstraw tangle of trees charred by a forest fire, the next I'm tripped up and flat on the ground, the canoe tossed aside and resting akimbo with an aspen branch penetrating its hull in a gruesome wound of splintered cedar. My beautiful 17-foot prospector canoe cannot express its pain, so I cry for it. With campsites few in this singed forest, daylight waning and a thunderstorm on its way, I wonder how long it will take to fix the hole and get back on the water.

My wife, Kim, and I are 10 days into a monthlong canoe trip on northern Ontario's Albany River with our friends Etienne and Maxime, a couple from Quebec. We're a curious foursome, having met online and never paddled or camped together before. Kim and I are sea kayak guides, dedicated low-impact campers most familiar with modern-day, "indestructible" equipment. Until now, we've always cooked on gas stoves, pitched nylon tents, and navigated whitewater rapids in canoes made of ABS plastic. Etienne, on the other hand, is a renaissance man. By day, he wears a tux and plays upright bass in the Quebec Symphony Orchestra. But his true avocation is traveling in the bush as traditionally as possible. He and Maxime paddle canvas canoes with beavertail blades, and sleep on tanned caribou skins in a woodstove-heated cotton tent. They pack their gear in cloth duffels and food in a wooden grub box known as a wannigan.

Kim has secretly started calling him Etienne Brulé, after the early French explorer who was among the first Europeans to venture into the Canadian hinterlands. In many regards, the moniker isn't far off. As we get to know him, we learn that Etienne and a friend once paddled and portaged 30 days across the wilds of northern Quebec with little more than a bag of flour, fishing rods and a shotgun to kill any geese or beaver they encountered on the trail. ("When you came back you were *so* skinny," laughs Maxime.) Yet Etienne scoffs at the notion of being a throwback. To him, fire irons, reflector ovens, axes and tumplines are avant-garde. "Plus, d'ere's no better sleeping pill d'an d'e smell of caribou skins," he says in his French-Canadian accent.

Kim balked at my suggestion that we also go old school on the Albany. "Tell him we'll pack food—no guns allowed," she implored. She conceded that as long as I carried it, we would paddle our beloved wood-canvas canoe. But she drew the line at a canvas tent and insisted we pack our food in waterproof plastic barrels with padded shoulder harnesses and hipbelts.

Now, Brulé assesses my busted canoe at the end of the portage. "No problem," he insists as I root through the repair kit in a panic. "Cover it with duct tape and we'll patch it up good tomorrow morning."

With that, Etienne and Maxime take off downstream while I hastily tape up the thumb-sized hole in the canoe's canvas skin, and push the splintered planking back in place. We haul our gear over another short portage just downstream before catching up with our trip mates at the head of a big rapid that billows with the telltale froth of holes and shallow rocks. We're exhausted and hungry, it's long past dinnertime, the sky is dark with anvil clouds and the shoreline's still burned to a crisp. It's a perfect time for another accident to occur, but there's no time to waste scouting the downstream run.

From shore, Etienne motions to a tongue of smooth-flowing water down the center. Kim turns around to settle Jack, our 65-pound husky mutt, in behind her seat in the bow of the canoe, and we drift hesitantly into the fray. She jabs her paddle manically while I call out the route from the stern, and the big, bruised canoe dances a dry line through the rapid without touching a rock. The small pool of water at my feet, I realize, is trickling in through the duct tape. I take a deep breath, just as I notice that the thunderheads have moved on.

Soon, the epic day ends on a heavily wooded knoll that somehow escaped the blaze.

∞

Months before in a string of emails, Etienne and I planned a canoe trip of nearly 400 miles through Canada's Little North. That's what 19th century fur traders called the 500,000 square-mile pentagon of wilderness bordered by the 50th parallel, Ontario's James and Hudson bay coastlines, and the province of Manitoba's Lake Winnipeg. On a map, the area teems alluringly with water—sprawling lakes like Savant, Seul and Big Trout, and countless river systems that eventually flow like capillaries into the Arctic sea—and is gloriously absent of roads and development. The majority of its human inhabitants are native Ojibwa and Cree who cling tenaciously to their traditional land in fly-in reserves. Big rivers like the Albany, Attawapiskat, Severn and Winisk are still highways, though most indigenous people have traded birchbark crafts for freighter canoes and tin boats powered with outboard motors.

We rendezvoused at the end of the road railway town of Nakina, Ontario. We stuffed canoes, gear and a month's worth of food in a Canadian National boxcar and rode the Trans-Canada train five hours west to the whistlestop at Flindt River, and unloaded at midnight on the side of the tracks. From here, we followed lakes, streams and ancient, well-worn portage trails to island-strewn Savant Lake, which took two days to transit.

Heading north, the intimately narrow yet powerful Savant River presented our first whitewater—short, fast-paced runs with just enough depth to pilot a canoe. We pulled ashore on glacier-smoothed granite, camped on sphagnum moss and reeled in pan-sized walleye from deep, dark pools.

We fell into a comfortable rhythm in camp. Upon landing each day, I'd locate a dead standing jack pine or spruce to cut up and split for firewood. Kim set up our tunnel-shaped nylon tent, and Etienne and Maxime worked on pitching their nine-by-nine cotton wall tent. Then Etienne would arrange rocks for the fire irons—metal rods used as pot supports for cooking. If the weather was nice, we'd go for a swim before starting dinner. Each couple alternated cooking days, so we were each responsible for 15 breakfasts and dinners. Every few evenings Etienne and I would engage in a rite of passage for traditional trippers—smearing fast-drying Ambroid cement on any dings or scratches on the fabric hulls of our canoes. And so I patched the hole in my prospector, cutting a piece of bandana, laminating it in place with cement and securing the busted cedar with five-minute epoxy.

On Day Nine the wily Pashkokogan River deposited us in the Albany, Ontario's longest watercourse, and we entered the remains of a massive 2011 wildfire that singed 250,000 acres of boreal forest to a charry crisp. We anticipated that reaching the big river would be a milestone, but instead it proved disappointing. Campsites and portages had been eradicated by the blaze, and we spent three days paddling through a depressing landscape of skeletal trees and bleached rock outcrops, wondering where we'd make camp for the night. Twice we were forced to hack out tentsites in thick bush, but eventually we escape the aftermath of the blaze and become enveloped in a sense of true wilderness.

"It feels like we've been out here for a long, long time," says Kim as we watch the sunset over the river on Day 14, making this the longest canoe trip of her life, "and we're only halfway done."

∞

About the same time it became normal for middle class North Americans to work weekends and multitask on smart phones, and when mortgages started to span lifetimes and average household debts entered six figures, extended canoe trips became a thing of the past. In the 1950s, Minnesotan writer Calvin Rutstrum would escape each summer for a spell in the Little North—seven weeks was about right. The late Canadian filmmaker, conservationist and canoe icon Bill Mason raved about the years he quit his job and paddled "from breakup to freeze-up." Canoeing guidebook author Kevin Callan notes that over the past three decades, however, the average canoe trip has decreased from 10 days to barely three.

Crowds at popular front-country parks like Minnesota's Boundary Waters Canoe Area and Ontario's Algonquin Provincial Park give the sense that canoe tripping is alive and well, but some argue the ranks of truly hard-core trippers are waning. According to my friend Hugh Stewart, the Quebec-based builder who crafted my prospector canoe, the end of serious tripping equates to the degeneration of outdoor skills. "You can get away with a lot of mistakes on a weekend trip," says Stewart, whose longest journey was a 10-week mission across the Canadian subarctic in 1980. "But on a long trip you really need to know what you're doing." Navigation, cooking, group dynamics—all these skills and more are tested and mastered on expeditions.

Then there are the profound social aspects of long-haul tripping. After a week on the water Kim and I know Etienne and Maxime like our best friends. Etienne and I discover that we can recite the entire scripts of Mason's *Path of the Paddle* films; the courses our lives have taken towards a passion for wilderness are strikingly similar. Maxime and Kim talk about grad school and the trips they've each made to Russia. Even Jack the dog makes a regular habit of taking a late afternoon nap in the canvas wall tent, swaddled in caribou furs with his new friends. Clearly, our relationships have progressed beyond online friends.

I hope the four of us—all well under 40 and without the strains of children or killer debt—represent a new generation of canoe trippers. Outfitters report that more and more young people are discovering backcountry tripping, and manufacturers and retailers are experiencing an uptick in canoe sales. There are others like us—freedom seekers like Winchell Delano, an American canoeist who has expeditioned across the breadth of the continent, including a west to east traverse of Canada's Yukon, Northwest and Nunavut territories and a south to north journey from the Gulf of Mexico to the Arctic Ocean. Traditional gear is also experiencing a resurgence: Hugh Stewart's Headwaters Canoes are in high demand; and summer youth camps such as Camp Temagami and Camp Keewaydin, both based in Ontario, outfit hard-core four- to seven-week expeditions on remote, whitewater rivers with wood-canvas canoes and old school gear. Perhaps we are, as Etienne likes to say, the vanguard of an old-school revolution.

∞

All along, we planned to take a rest day on Eabamet Lake, an expansive body of water adjacent to the native settlement of Fort Hope. From our campsite of Day 18 and 19 on Eabamet's south shore, the town of 1,000 looks like an idyllic cluster of houses and dusty streets radiating inland from a classic northern lake. We observed the village through binoculars, dreaming of ice cream and potato chips. Still, we paddled across the lake and into town with trepidation, nervous of our first human contact in weeks. We've heard stories of remote northern communities like this—mostly pertaining to rampant drug addiction, violence, suicide epidemics and poverty. The first thing we see upon landing are ramshackle bungalows tagged with graffiti and sooty from chimney fires, perpetuating the image of social dysfunction. Fort Hope's roads bustle with loose dogs, bicycling children and adults on all-terrain vehicles. Kim struggles as Jack strains excitedly at his leash and a group of kindergarten-aged girls gathers around Maxime. They clutch her hands with a stirring sense of innocence and examine her sketchbook with bright-eyed curiosity. "Will you be our new teacher?" they wonder.

Etienne and I sit down with an older man outside the grocery store. "Are you guys prospectors?" he asks, guardedly. He warms when we tell him we're canoeists. We probe him for information about Frenchman's Rapids, a drop located 20 miles downstream. "The portage is on the right," he says. Another man chimes in. "Don't listen to Louis," he chuckles. "I can run Frenchman's with my eyes closed! Watch the whirlpool at the top and stay to the left." They clearly know their traditional land intimately.

The man named Louis, however, would rather talk about mining and the future of Fort Hope. Amongst prospectors, mining companies and stock market speculators, this part of Ontario is known as the "Ring of Fire"—a 5,800 square-mile, crescent-shaped lode of nickel, copper and other minerals. Just north of here is a prospect that's said to be North America's richest find of chromite, a metal used in stainless steel, valued at a whopping $60 billion. Noront, a Toronto-based company, is working to build a mine. The development is contingent upon the construction of the region's first all-season road to bring workers in and ship ore out for processing in the south. Ostensibly, the plan has the full support of the provincial government, which has called the Ring of Fire "the most promising mining opportunity in years." Government set a precedent by green-lighting a de Beers diamond mine near the James Bay coast that's been operational since 2008. The Little North, it seems, is open for business.

Locals like Louis, however, aren't so sure. While de Beers' Victor mine promised to prioritize First Nations workers, Louis claims the company cherry-picked trained aboriginal employees from outside of the region. The nearby native village of Attawapiskat, meanwhile, regularly makes national headlines for its Third World-like housing crisis and condemned elementary school that sits atop diesel-contaminated soil. What's more, de Beers suddenly announced it will mothball the Victor mine in 2019, leaving a massive crater in the muskeg and withdrawing any economic gains it brought to the area.

Meanwhile, First Nations are getting tired of being duped. Communities have become more assertive of their rights to the lands they've occupied for 8,000 years, arguing for a bigger stake in decision-making. Some chiefs have gone so far as to pledge to block development altogether. "Once there is a permanent access road, our way of life will be changed forever," announced Peter Moonias, the former chief of Neskantaga First Nation, an Oji-Cree community located 45 miles north of Fort Hope on the doorstep of the Ring of Fire mining claims. "We will not be able to turn back the clock."

In Fort Hope, Louis says geologists whisked in by helicopter have literally surrounded the reserve with claim stakes. He rubs his chin thoughtfully and shakes his head in disbelief. "We're sitting on a gold mine," he says. "It should be our decision on how it gets developed."

That night, Kim and I stay up late and reflect upon the day. We're throwbacks not only for our choice of old-fashioned canoes and monthlong trip, but also for the way we're experiencing a fast-fading way of life. We lament the loss of the Old North, but of course we must balance this sense of heartbreak with our own dependence on commerce and technology. It's a dilemma that's as difficult to reconcile as the choice a man like Louis faces in allowing or prohibiting miners on his birthright lands.

In Cree mythology, the pulsing northern lights are the spirits of the elders, dancing across the sky. Later on, it feels strangely prescient when we awaken to watch the aurora shimmering bright over Eabamet Lake and pallid streetlights of Fort Hope.

∞

Another day on the river, and I'm watching three ravens wheeling above the spruce treetops, subtly ruddering their tail feathers to maneuver in the same way we angle our paddles to deke through rapids. As the days turned to weeks, we see the birch trees turn russet with the approach of autumn. The ground beneath our feet has come alive with toads, spiders, ants and insects. We spot moose from impossible distances, and have figured out how to train our lures on tasty walleye instead of boney pike. We're getting to know a subtle yet rich landscape that's been described as a "stronghold of biodiversity" and "one of the world's largest, most intact ecological systems" by scientists.

Most noticeable is how the Albany itself has become as familiar as an old friend. We've felt it grow in width and volume and become adept at judging the depth of rocks in its tea-stained clarity. We haven't pulled out the Ambroid to patch the canoe in days. By the time we reach Frenchman's, a long, powerful rapid with surging waves and swirling eddies, we're well-acquainted with the Albany's mannerisms when the riverbed trends downhill.

Given the time, we could've spent an entire day running and re-running Frenchman's Rapids. After a bouldery start, the river narrows and funnels into a series of step-ledges and recirculating holes at breakneck speed. The trick is—as we were advised in Fort Hope—to stay left, venturing into the river-center wave train just enough for a little excitement. The weeklong section between Fort Hope and our seaplane take-out at the First Nations community of Ogoki Post is replete with whitewater thrills, from the countless gravel swifts to the complex series of whitewater rapids at Kagiami Falls.

Kim and I never expected this sort of high-adventure, high-stakes paddling—both in our choice of a seemingly fragile canoe and our decision to travel with Jack, our bush savvy but young and excitable dog. Yet both fare remarkably well: The responsive and voluminous prospector hull is ideally suited to the large waves and deep channels of the Albany's rapids, and Jack learns to sit still in the canoe—or to wait for us on shore when things get big and dicey. All too soon the whitewater run ends at Marten Falls, where the river spills off the northern edge of the Canadian Shield and we camp for the second-last night on stalwart granite. From here, the Albany's flow cuts across a muskeg halo that extends inland from James Bay—a huge, predominantly wetlands complex comparable in size to the Amazon.

About now it seems like we should slow down. But on our final full day on the river we cover an easy 30 miles in unfailing current. The sky darkens as we make camp atop a steep island of limestone rubble that's dotted with bear tracks. There's a native trap cabin tucked into the black spruce on the mainland across the channel; we watch as a couple arrives by motorized canoe from downriver after dinner and pulls into the reedy shore. It's a final opportunity for us to bear witness to a scene from the past. The sun breaks momentarily through the clouds like a ball of copper, a flock of geese lands on the river, and a single shotgun blast breaks the silence.

Soon, this landscape could very well be bisected with roads and dug up with mines. Just as likely, the rapids and falls of the Albany River tapped for hydroelectricity to feed an industrial juggernaut. Tonight, though, time stands still. Our neighbors on the river will eat well.

THE LONER

James Roberts

You can see the source of the Monk's Pool from a distance, a stain of deep green bleeding out from the brown, a horse shoe indentation in the slope. Water bubbles out of the ground from a little cup sized puddle which overflows into a stream so narrow the grass obscures it for most of its short journey down this Welsh hillside. The stream reveals the poverty of the soil here, its centuries of journeying having eroded only a few inches of the turf to a bed of mudstone. Bracken and gorse carpet the hill with, here and there, the odd thorn tree, split, wind-twisted and brittle. The pool was once edged with a line of Scots Pine but the level of the water was raised in recent times, flooding the roots of most of the trees which are now bare, bleached crucifixes.

Mid winter. The pool is usually empty at this time of cold sleep. But this has been a year of anomalies and it is inhabited now by a single juvenile mute swan. A mile south the potato crop has been harvested and the sheltered fields next to the river are starting to fill up with swans, hundreds of birds, many having migrated here from as far as Scandinavia. It is an old gathering place that all the swans in the region come to. Except for the single loner fifteen hundred feet up, facing a much harsher winter.

The cob and pen arrived in early March, circling the pool over the spring passage flocks of teal and mallard, resident coots and moorhens. Small groups of Canada geese started landing soon afterwards. Almost as soon as the birds had settled the cob attacked, neck extended, head low, skidding towards them, air screaming over its wings. The geese took off, territory conceded. Later that week the swans began to build their nest inside an oval of bullrushes. Soon the pen was sitting on seven eggs while the cob defended the territory against every potential predator including the otter that started to leave its spraints on the boulders while it waited for the annual arrival of toads to their breeding ground at the pool's shallow edges.

Six of the seven eggs hatched in early May with the first swallows arcing over the water and the sound of a pair of curlews off to the west where they were nesting near the stream. For the coming weeks the tiny cygnets would be guided around the lake by their parents, travelling single file with pen leading and cob guarding the rear unless a walker happened to stop, when the cob would paddle towards them hissing. At this time an ancient, battered old tractor started to appear by the pool, parked alongside the reed bed where the nest still held one beige egg that had not hatched. I walked up to it and an old farmer flung open the cab door. He was dressed in a wax jacket and hat that were almost rags. Inside was a sheepdog chained to the door, its teeth bared, doing its best to savage me until the farmer shouted it down. He told me he has farmed on the hill for seventy years and this was the first time he'd ever seen swans breed on the pool.

Because they are a regular sight on urban waterways mute swans are regarded as a common bird in the UK. But the population is actually quite sparse, with only around 7,000 breeding pairs. Compare this to the 100,000 pairs of mallards or the 60,000 pairs of Canada geese. An average year produces only about 3,500 successfully reared cygnets. It is possible that this was the first time swans had ever bred here.

My first experience of a wild pool was near the North Midlands housing estate where I grew up. It was located behind an old priory and had once been a mill pond, the mill itself long demolished. The pool was almost identical to the Monk's Pool in size, though instead of being surrounded by a thousand acres of heath, it was hemmed in by a similar acreage of council houses and overlooked by a twenty storey block of flats. The pond was fed by an underground spring which trickled out from a steep embankment at its north end. It was a ghost of rural life lingering in the industrial suburban spread, managing to maintain a wild community. The water was always swarming with sticklebacks in summer and we all knew a monster pike lurked in its trenches, some of us having had the good fortune to hook it while never managing to land it. A large, bordering willow had fallen into the pond and regrown. Within a fork in its horizontal trunk was the swans' nest.

Every summer there were cygnets on the pond, such a regular feature I hardly noticed them. As I reached my teens, deindustrialisation began and the pond mirrored the decline of its surroundings. The spring seemed to dry up for long periods and the water became stagnant, carpeted with slime I could smell all the way from my garden. Litter started to appear, at first the odd glass bottle thrown into the water, then, as packaging plastics began to be used more frequently the surrounding trees filled up with coloured bags that draped from the branches like dead sea creatures. The swans bred less and less successfully and eventually stopped breeding altogether, only using the pond as an occasional stop-off point. The decades old nest filled up with litter. The water is almost lifeless now, the surrounding paths strewn with smashed glass, dangerous for wildlife and people. The last time I visited the area was being menaced by a lone cob which had lost its mate. It threatened anyone who passed, wings thrashing, hissing, grief transformed into aggression.

Swans are one of the heaviest of flying birds. The serene white creature that, on water, moves without moving, its neck sinuous as a river, has to batter itself aloft. It needs an enormous amount of space to do this. The Monk's Pool is barely large enough to allow a successful take off, requiring the bird to begin its ascent at the edge of the water and to aim itself at the gaps between the fringe of trees and bushes. It takes a full ten seconds of thrashing across the water, feet scrabbling for propulsion, wingtips slapping the surface, before a few feet of altitude is attained. Once in the air it is a noisy machine, the rapid thrum of its wingbeats drowning out the surrounding birdsong. They are not skilful flyers. In the early autumn winds I watched a pair make a wide and slow circle of the hill before navigating a route to the pool. They then became stuck as they attempted to land into the wind, suspended twenty feet above the water, moving slowly backwards. In the end they gave up and turned towards the river below and shelter from the westerly. They were replaced by a lone red kite tilting, tail fanned, wings motionless as it slid through the cracks in the gale.

Throughout the summer the swans continued to patrol the pool in military formation. The pen pulled up weeds from the pool bed and dropped them onto the surface of the water for the cygnets to pick at daintily. They made continual, barely audible, whistling calls. They doubled in size every few weeks. By early July the cob had let down his guard a little and had begun to wander around the pool away from the family while the cygnets travelled in a cluster, following the pen but not closely. Then, one morning, the cob was gone. I searched for hours in the reeds and surrounding bracken for signs of predation. There were none. The pen didn't seem too concerned; she attended to her young as normal. Swans are one of many species of bird that pair for life but, as with humans, separations occur. Guillemots have been studied closely in this regard and it has been found that most separations are due to bad parenting. In these cases the deviant bird is aggressively seen off. I'm sure this was not the case with the swans. There were no signs of aggression by the cob to its young and I never saw the pen attempt to drive off its mate. The cob just left.

Mute swans can hold their territories with incredible tenacity even when those territories are unsuitable. On the river Wye, below the road bridge leading into town a low island of reeds and hazel separates the stream into a fork. A pair of swans have nested in this place every year I have lived here. In April heavy rains begin and the Wye, being a shallow, mountain river, rises rapidly until only the tops of the hazels show, the nest drowned and destroyed, the unhatched eggs washed away. It doesn't deter them, the next year they begin again. Only this year, in a spring of little rainfall, have they succeeded in raising young. The pair were still on their patch of river in early winter with their three juveniles in tow.

Anomalous behaviour in wild animals is not rare. Anyone who spends a lot of time observing the natural world will come across unusual behaviour. As the writer Neil Ansell states in his book "Deep Country", watching wildlife over long periods of time is like peeling an onion, you penetrate through to layer after layer of ever more complex behaviour. Mute Swans are huge birds and voracious eaters. They can consume up to 8 pounds of vegetation each day. Monk's Pool is less than an acre in area. It is my guess that the cob left its territory so the young had an ample supply of food for the rest of their dependent stage.

"The Six Swans" is a well known oral story with variants across Germany and Scandinavia. In the tale a king gets lost hunting in the forest and meets a witch who will only agree to show him the way back to his castle if he takes her daughter as a wife. The king reluctantly agrees and marries the daughter on his return. But, though his bride is beautiful, he does not trust her. He removes his children from the castle and takes them to a place where they will be hidden from their stepmother. The new queen grows suspicious and eventually finds the hidden place. When she visits it the six boys, believing her to be their father arriving, run out to greet her. The witch stepmother then turns each of them into swans. But she does not discover the seventh child, the boys' sister. The abandoned sister searches the wild forest until she finds her swan brothers who are cursed to only be able to throw off their feathers and become human for a few minutes each day. The only way she can give them back their forms permanently is to make no sound for six years and to weave each brother a shirt of starwort. This she promises to do. The girl is then discovered in the forest by another king who falls in love with her and they marry. But the girl has inherited another wicked guardian and each time she bears a child the old woman steals it and marks the young mother's lips with blood, accusing her of devouring her own child. The girl is mute and cannot defend herself but the king does not believe his mother. Eventually after their third child receives the same fate, the king can defend his wife no more and she is condemned to burn at the stake. But by now six years have passed and she has woven the shirts of starwort except for a single sleeve. As the pyre is about to be set alight six swans swoop down to her and she throws a shirt over each one. The swans are transformed back to her brothers, one with a white wing in place of an arm. The sister can finally tell the truth and the king's mother is forced to reveal where the children are hidden, after which she is burned to ashes.

The story was first written down by Jacob and Wilhelm Grimm. It was one of their favourite tales because of its theme of family fidelity. The detail that seems most strange about the story is the single white wing left in place of the brother's arm. I think it is a reminder of the faithfulness of creatures that the surrounding presence of wild beings teaches and inspires us and should not be forgotten or dismissed.

The moult began in late summer, feathers rimming the pool forming a random, pale tideline. The cygnets were by now almost the size of the pen though they still followed their mother everywhere. Their infant calls remained, the continual shy "seep" that now seemed incongruous with their size. Weeks later, with the first heavy dew settling and the ends of the bracken fronds curling and brown, the pen began flying lessons, spreading and beating its wings in front of them and then launching itself across the pool. The cygnets began to rear out of the water and test the strength of their own wings.

On a late September morning I arrived just after dawn to see the pen and only four cygnets. A few days later, there were two. Then, on a day when the first mist blurred the whole valley, I looked over a silver oval of water now empty of swans. I walked down to the nest, still perfectly intact inside its moat, with the single unhatched egg still undisturbed. I collected a few white feathers from among the reeds while a pair of ravens flipped and circled over the row of drowned pines. And then I heard, close by, the call of a cygnet and looked up to see it bending and poking among the bulrushes. One had stayed. Over the following weeks the pen returned many times to try to guide its youngster away from the pool. Sometimes it stayed for a day, other times three or four but each time the pen left and the gaps between visits became longer. The juvenile refused to leave.

For a whole month storms have been raging, gale force winds ravaging the peaks, ripping weak branches from the thorn trees and scouring the dead bracken. The upland is scattered with sulphur tufts and scarlet caps like tiny fires amongst the star moss and sedge. A flock of fieldfares cleared the last berries from the neglected hedges but now they have moved on, leaving the hill to a pair of red kites who will hunt here all winter. A few crows and ravens hang out in the tree skeletons, slinging insults. Occasionally I spot a kestrel hovering above the scrub where the curlews nested. The hill is almost deserted. The Monk's Pool is a cold eye peering out of the barren landscape, the young swan its only inhabitant, now struggling with the conditions.

A week ago the temperature dropped and the ground froze hard. The pool became a giant cobweb of ice. The sun rises almost from the south now, beginning its shallow arc clearing the long line of whaleback mountains for the few hours before dark. In the red, dawn light I could see the long necked silhouette of the swan out in the middle of the pool. It struggled to get though the ice, trying to climb out, falling through, trying to peck its way forwards. Then it opened its wings and I saw how stunted they were, unable to lift it even a few inches from the surface. Its voice had finally changed. While it struggled it made the low, plaintive, and rarely heard call of the mature swan.

After the short cold snap another series of more violent storms blew in. Howling wind and torrential rain lasted all week and I did not make it onto the hill until this morning. Under the shut sky the pool was edged with grey foam, the water still cresting, the reeds slapped flat. The swan was not there. Heading back to the road I saw two ravens flip-diving in the last of the wind eddies and went to stand under them. As I turned for home, I noticed something pale amongst the sedge. It was a patch of skin the size of my palm, coated with white feathers.

As well as swan stories, there are many Welsh oral tales involving upland pools. They are the places where magical creatures are conjured from the water to spend a time living with mortals. But the beautiful beings are always in some way, injured by life. They return to their pools, dive, and are never seen again.

THREE RIVERS

Karen Lloyd

We bought our house on the edge of the English Lake District because we had been beguiled by the view. From our upstairs windows, the outlook north is to the Kentmere mountains, and they are our barometer of the weather. When the weather turns cold, winter's first frostings define the mountain ridge of Froswick, Ill Bell and Yoke. In summer, as the setting sun falls below the fells, our long equinoctial evenings acquire an ageless citrine glow. A short walk across the road and up the footpath through fields to the open vantage point of Kendal Fell, you can trace the shape that the River Kent forges through the landscape. The Kent is a short river; only twenty miles pass from its wellspring below the headwall of Mardale Ill Bell to its outfall into Morecambe Bay. In its early life, the Kent flowed through the crag-bound upper valley, passing an invocation of Cumbrian place names; Rainsborrow Cove, Green Quarter, Withered Howe, Elf Howe.

Underneath the rock-terraces of Castle Crag, the Kent is muscular and bouldered. It forges a headlong rush towards Force Jump Waterfall before it turns towards a wider landscape and passes through a litany of woodlands, Craggy Wood, Dorothy Farrer's Wood and Spring Hagg.

Under the dome of indigenous trees in May, the world turns beneath slopes and slews of cobalt—the particular shade of blue of our most prolific native wildflower, the bluebell. Come on a slow-bright evening, it is as if the earth hums with blue; the blue of distance and memory. In Beck Mickle Ing Wood the riverbanks are lined with ancient coppiced hazel trees; numerous trunks rise like masts from immense horizontal trunks. Many trees of one tree, they are like galleons beached at low tide. Come after heavy rain, and you can hear the river talking as it sifts and grades its stones and cobbles. Turn stones slowly in the shallows and you might find crayfish. Once disturbed, with an almighty kick of their antediluvian, articulated tails, they are spirited away into the riverbed.

The Kent flows on through fields and farmland and on through the centre of Kendal, spanned by road bridges and footbridges, from where in the summer you might spot a local otter feeding her kits, or in the quieter stretches, a pair of ringed plover, agitated and edgy, guarding a hidden nest.

Looking north from Kendal Fell, the valley beyond the Kent is that of Longsleddale, and here, at almost two thousand feet high, the River Sprint is born; what better name for England's fastest rising river? The Sprint appears under the summit ridge of Harter Fell where the peat breaks into a couple of dark runnels. The stream quickly gains momentum, turning out of a blind valley and rapidly becoming a clear-running beck that bustles over grey and white, black-as-jet and rusty-red stones. It plunges over small cascades and crashes at breakneck speed into and out of the deserted slate quarries of Wrengill where the archaeology of slate workings and quarrymen's roofless cottages remain as testament to the Lake District's industrial past. Further down the fellside the Sprint veers south-east to fall and twist and fall again in a series of cascades that gush and crash whenever the river is in spate. It runs alongside the steep climb of Gatesgarth Pass, one of the ancient packhorse routes connecting north to south, and where native Cumbrian Fell ponies once carried woollen goods and food towards the markets of Kendal and beyond, following each other through thick mist by the dull monotony of harness bells. And the river too, would have formed an underscore to the trudge of the ponies' hooves and the boots of their people.

Mountain shadows fall early here: Kentmere Pike, Steel Rigg, Raven Crag, Goat Scar and Shipman Knotts. The Sprint falls further, washing over gravel beds before singing itself underneath the packhorse bridge by Sadgill farm and ploughing onwards through the fields of Longsleddale. That word *dale,* scattered as it is throughout the Lake District, is indicative of a Norse past. Our Viking ancestors remained long enough to allow landscape and language to be forged together, to become symbiotic. You can find the derivation of that language on any local map – *fors*, waterfall, or force; *fjall,* fell; *gil*, or gill—a ravine; *beckr,* a stream or beck; *tjorn,* a small lake, a tarn. Underneath the curlew-sung slopes of Potter Fell the Sprint takes a westward swing beyond Garnett Bridge, and eventually moves clear of the fells to where Kendal becomes visible a few miles distant, and beyond the town, Morecambe Bay, shining at full tide like a ragged shield. The river carries itself along towards Oak Bank and Sprint Mill and a mile further, gives itself up to the greater flow of the Kent.

The river Mint comes from an altogether quieter place. The next valley north again is Bannisdale—a name that even locals might have heard of, but would be hard pressed to locate. But I like this, the obscurity of it, and how, whenever I go there, apart from the farmers at Dry Howe, there's rarely anyone about. The single-track lane into the valley is set between parallel drystone walls and after a couple of miles drops over the shoulder of the fellside where the farm comes into view, a no-nonsense affair with a white-painted farmhouse, shippons for cows and barns for storing sileage. As valleys go, Bannisdale is short, perhaps less than three miles from the road-head to the head of the valley where the gill tumbles alongside a path into the hills. At the end of the track, hidden from view for all but the last half mile, there's a single white-painted cottage, the place where the shepherd from the farm used to live, then a couple who wanted to get away from it all, until they'd got away for too long and moved closer to civilisation. These days it's a holiday cottage, and rarely used.

The encircling hills offer a quality of quietness that belies the mere handful of miles back to town. Bannisdale is neither a brash nor a boastful place. There are no towering peaks or crashing waterfalls. No elegant languorous rivers following the slow beat of geology. Just the path and the farm, the fellsides, a few crags and the infant Mint. Hunting buzzards contour the fellside and a kestrel perhaps, hanging on air, moving on again in an elegant curve, high and pale like a floater moving over an iris. The place names too are quieter; Whiteside Pike, Todd Fell, White Howe, Lamb Pasture. Bannisdale is a valley to be on more intimate terms with, more human scale. Look on the map and a series of ancient enclosures are marked, the dwellings and stock enclosures of people who settled here some 8,000 years ago. Early pastoralists, they had begun to settle, leaving behind the hunter-gatherer way of life, and beginning to clear the land for crops and to keep a few animals. Close on the heels of the last Ice Age, the landscape these people would have known was not what we might at first imagine. At this point, forest cover had yet to arrive. What would have been here was a scrubby cover of birch and heathers and juniper. The settlers felled timber for fuel, but with their hand axes and other primitive tools, their ability to impact upon a whole landscape system should not be over-stated.

Half way along the valley, the Mint sweeps west, following an unlikely route, disappearing on the far side of a drystone wall and eventually butting up against the slope of the fell—an unnatural place for a river, if ever there was one. In front of the wall is a large flat area of juncus grass, beloved plant of wet places, stretching for a quarter of a mile further into the valley. This was the tarn of Dub Ings, until it was drained in some previous attempt to create yet more grazing for sheep. Diverting the beck to run past, rather than through the tarn, has reduced it to a dried-out expanse, the juncus spreading out as an ochre lake, devoid of water.

∞

The three valleys and their rivers are for me, and many like me, places to retreat to, to escape from the everyday, places to walk and think and be. But as well as offering retreat and solace, the rivers can and do wreak havoc on the rural landscape and on the larger communities downstream.

On 5th December 2016, Storm Desmond came to call. In less than twenty-four hours, 15 trillion litres of rain poured down on Cumbria and neighbouring north Lancashire. Siren after siren blared past our house on the way to one disaster after another. We listened to the radio and watched news reports coming in. One after another, the county's bridges were being reduced to rubble underneath the weight of water.

'Scroggs Bridge in Kentmere has gone.'

'There's no way in or out of Levens village.'

'People are stranded on the road at Heversham.'

'The A591 is under water.'

'Appleby Bridge has gone.'

In the afternoon, my son Callum and I set off into town. We were prepared for a soaking, though I'd never previously known rain to break an umbrella. At the back of the local police station, the Kent had breached its banks in bewildering fashion, drowning the wide riverside path, and was about to annexe the wide spaces of the police station car park. A white car was already half submerged, and water lapped at the wheel rims of others. The skate park and fields on the opposite bank had disappeared.

As we walked towards the centre of Kendal, we saw the river behaving in ways that we had never seen, and never wish to see again. One of the footbridges, had become adrift mid-flood, unpurposed. Traffic did not move because there were no routes open. And there was a strange backdrop of soundlessness; just the brown torrent careering on. Roiling, you might have said. We took in the shock and drama of it. Over 2,000 homes were flooded in this town alone that day. Lives were being turned upside down.

We walked back up the hill towards our house, though the road was now more like a river. Gravel and earth had been scoured from the fell and from gardens and were being deposited like new shingle beds on the tarmac. News bulletins urged *'stay home'*, *'don't go anywhere—the emergency services are struggling'*. From these minute by minute reports we took in the scale of the impact as Storm Desmond passed over, drowning a whole county and more—into the cities of Lancaster and Carlisle, where thousands more were made homeless. Forget history; this was history. Then the lights went out as electricity substations became swimming pools, and misery spread as thickly as the rain. Between Grasmere and Keswick, a mountainside collapsed, and the force of rainwater broke the road apart, creating a 140-mile round trip commute for those whose daily lives involved travelling between the two towns.

Out there, in the fading unnatural daylight and the ruin of failed electric light, the Sprint and the Mint were being force-fed by biblical volumes of rain. To the immediate north of Kendal, one after another the rivers merge with the Kent, and it was there on the outskirts, in the edgelands of industrial estates, rugby fields and shopping centres that this unprecedented, disinhibited rain came canyoning along, merging together in an almighty confluence, and began to breach—picking up timber, oil, sewage and chemicals and pouring on towards the town, into housing estates where streets became grubby rivers and cellars filled with filthy water and ground floors were subsumed up to shoulder height.

And what about the otters I had thought? Their riverside holts inundated, how far would they have to travel, to get away? Do they need to get away? What does a flood like this do to the wildlife of a river system, to the goosanders and fish, the mallards and the gulls? What was this annihilating weather doing to them?

∞

In the autumn of 2017, at that point in the year when the sense of the earth shifting down a gear is tangible, I walked into Bannisdale with Simon Stainer, a lead advisor and ecologist with the government's adviser for the *natural* environment, Natural England. I like walking with ecologists. I like the way the conversation rambles and focusses as we move through the landscape, and how the subjects of which we speak are here in front of us. Twice now, Simon has taken me to look at trees, or the places where trees will soon be. As we walked, we talked about rivers and rainfall. And for us, it is no longer possible to talk about the Lake District and its rivers without talking about the mountains and fellsides of the place we both call home. And we needed to talk about trees.

We parked the car and set off. There was a gate to be opened and as it clanged shut, a farm dog barked. Beneath a small humpback bridge the incipient River Mint gurgled, running clear or forming unfathomable peat-black pools. The morning had been wet—yet again—and after four unseasonable months of rain, what foliage remained in the sprawling remnants of an alder wood on the fellside above the farm, was dull and uniformly brown, as if the trees themselves had given up any claim to the season at hand. Further on, the fellsides were scattered with occasional hawthorns.

The sky was temperamental. It threw down sharp showers and I pulled up my hood and put my notebook and pen away in my pocket until the squall passed. Then the clouds broke apart and over the span of the valley, stretching from fellside to fellside, a perfect rainbow evolved. Underneath the centre of the arc, a few rumple-headed ash trees and a leviathan oak were some of the small number of trees that remained in the valley.

'When you see a lone tree in the landscape,' Simon said, indicating the hills surrounding us, 'an old hawthorn or a Scots Pine, what it represents is the loss of tree-cover on a monumental scale. Every generation assumes that what they are looking at is 'normal.' But without the planting of new trees, these veteran trees will continue to die away with nothing to replace them. And with trees, he went on, 'comes bio-diversity—the increase of life, of invertebrates and birds and mammals.'

Take a look at an aerial map of the Lake District. See how little of the land is codified green, for woodland or forest. Larger areas will undoubtedly be that of forestry, planted for timber, but where indigenous tree cover does exist, those tiny green spaces on the map are as sparse and insignificant as the dried up algal pools of a river in drought.

This winter, in a scheme designed to combine increasing bio-diversity with attenuation—or natural flood defence—the nature of the landscape in Bannisdale is under the process of change. Thousands of trees are being planted below Capplefall Crags and on the fellside above Dry Howe farm. Two local farming families are working in schemes supported by Natural England to reduce the numbers of sheep on the fells, and to restrict the grazing area through the installation of new fencing, so that the new trees can become established.

As we walked, we heard the intermittent buzz of machinery. An all-terrain vehicle was transporting bundles of stakes onto the slopes, and on the track below, a land-rover had been piled high with stripling native trees. In the coming years there will be an incipient cover of birch—that great coloniser, and holly, hawthorn, rowan, oak, alder and aspen covering three hundred hectares of ground. And next summer, 50,000 more hawthorns will be planted to create indigenous wood pasture, creating a natural mosaic of tree cover and open ground. The new tree-scape will take time to evolve, but with it will come numerous niches and habitats for an increasing number of species.

I remembered our last walk together, when we had climbed up into Wordsworth territory, into the steep valleys of Scandale and Rydal in the central Lakes, and where long horn cattle had recently been substituted for the sheep – cows that graze and move on more quickly, and whose heavy hooves break open the ground to allow seeds to fall and germinate. 'Once the sheep are removed,' Simon had told me as we climbed, 'some of our most rarely found and exceptional native wild flowers will come back. They're always there in the ground, but the sheep move slowly, eating everything in their path.' And as if to illustrate the point, we turned away from the path and headed up onto the fellside towards an outcrop of rocks, and there we saw, growing like an outsize bonsai, a rowan tree growing from a crack in the stone. Then Simon spotted something else. He scrambled closer to the rocks and took hold of a trailing plant. 'This bramble is coming back simply because the sheep have been taken off the hill. And look—here's a seedling ash tree.' A tiny tree, sprouting from a slender fissure in the rock.

High on the exposed fellside above the Vale of Rydal, scattered in a wet flush where rainwater drains away following the natural lie of the land, Simon found clusters of birds-eye primroses, a flower I had never seen before, in all my years of walking the fells. It was pale pink and star-like, growing amidst the tough and yellowed grasses. 'If the sheep were still here, he said, 'these would have been eaten away.' Both Rydal and Scandale have been planted up with thousands of native trees. Protected by sturdy wooden palisades or by plastic tubes, they cover the fellsides. A future forest, growing over the valley slopes and the high fellsides up to where the blanket bracken cover fades away, and bracken is a genetic marker that illustrates the extent of tree cover in the past. The effect of the new tree plantings is already staggering. Imagine then, in a decade's time, how that incipient forest will flicker red and gold in autumn, bringing the fellsides to life again.

I couldn't begin to think how to re-imagine a river. But along with the tree-planting, the beck in Bannisdale will be given back its natural life. Previous centuries had seen attempts to straighten, or canalise the beck, but now it will be re-gifted its meandering form, so that the curves and lazy bends can behave in the way they are supposed to, to naturally slow the flow. And the dead tarn too, will be given back its life and its water, and this river-fed soakaway will also help to slow down our increasingly unnaturally rainfall. This will be climate-change action at work, albeit in an unknown valley in a quiet corner of the north of England.

'In the aftermath of Storm Desmond,' Simon said, 'the boffins who sit in their offices and do their sums worked out that if the Mint had been running its original, un-straightened course, and if the tarn had been wet and capable of absorbing more rainwater off the fellsides, and if the fells had been covered in trees, the full force of the volume of water in the river Mint would have been delayed by eleven hours. That means that all those people and houses and businesses in Kendal would not have suffered such extensive flooding. It's a no brainer.'

We turned to walk back out of the valley, and in the way of these things, the view became changed. And my view too, had become altered. Part of the answer at least, to climate change here in the north, is in allowing our rivers to do what they do best – to carry away exceptional volumes of water with the least damage to the land – and to its people.

∞

You don't see Sprint Mill from the road. You don't see it unless you take a hike across the fields and follow the Dales Way long-distance walking path, and placed at an elegant bend in the river, is a house and the mill. From here, the footpath dives into a fringe of wooded river margins, and before long you arrive at a slant-wise waterfall, and below this, as if placed there to provide what the Victorians liked to call 'viewing stations,' an elongated spur of rock juts out from the bank into the river. Sitting here is as good a place as any from which to contemplate the aesthetics of a Lake District river. The sibilance of running water, the intermittent clear pools that fall fifteen feet deep and where, if you had a mind, you could count every single rock and cobble on the river-bed. The Cumbrian poet Kerry Darbishire described the sheer edges here, and the geological processes inherent in them as 'great blue slabs/ of fallen books.' In May, the curling viridian leaf spears of ramsons, or wild garlic, are bursting with white star-flowers. Walking the narrow path, the scent of garlic rises and catches on the in-breath. There will be blackbirds busy with summer's work, parties of wrens like small ticking clocks amongst the holly, and foraging parties of long-tailed tits, their sociable high-pitched chatter preceding the sight of them as they move constantly amongst the high branches.

The photographer Florence Acland grew up at Sprint Mill. As kids, she and her two brothers spent their summers swimming and crawling up-river, climbing the small water-shoots and pushing up against the slantwise falls to gain the shallower, slower-flowing river bed from where it is but a short riverine scramble along to Oak Bank – another former mill, converted to cottages that are surrounded by gardens and chickens and the buzz of bees. In one form or another, a mill has existed at this bend in the River Sprint since the 1400's; the valley and much of the surrounding countryside has a rich association with wool production. Shakespeare includes not one, but three references to 'Kendal green' – the shade of woollen cloth produced in the valleys surrounding the town.

Until the 1960's, horse blankets and rough woven cloth were produced at Sprint Mill by whatever mechanical means the river aided. For the past thirty years, Florence's father, Edward Acland, has re-visioned, or re-invented the mill. He has become a collector of ephemera and a noticer of the unsung. Glass jars are arranged on shelves. They contain the objects that others would overlook or discard; the nests of mice, nails fallen from burning firewood and collected from ashes at the bottom of the stove, wristwatch and clock parts—springs and casings and faces, the skeletal remains of physallis cases, the strangely sci-fi-looking pods of Cape Gooseberry, baler twine, sea-polished coloured stones from Hebridean beaches, damson stones that have been chiselled by the teeth of voles, leaving perfect holes at their centre. And through the making of assemblages and then photographing them, he and Flo make pieces of art that are unlike anything else. One of the most striking (though I hesitate to use the word,) is 'Timepiece.' At the centre of the image is an antique brass fob watch encircled by dying ox eye daisies, and around this an encircling ring made up of the miniature figures of a brass band, red-jacketed and bow tied, interspersed with thistle seeds, old-fashioned brass bell-pushes, melon seeds. The band beats out the time, but time has its own purpose, its own disposition, its own inevitability.

Outside are vegetable gardens, bee hives, goats and chickens and ducks. An orchard of historic varieties of apples and pears and damsons—*Howgate Wonder, Keswick Codlin, James Grieve.* Edward talks about his philosophy of *Guardening*, of taking care of the land, of how we should all take notice, and place a greater emphasis of care on what it is that we do, and how it is that we live.

∞

As I write, the second anniversary of Storm Desmond has recently passed, though it went unremarked in the national press. And why should it have? The answer lies in the 242 road or foot-bridges that are yet to be re-opened in Cumbria, out of 784 bridges that were undermined and made unfit for use, as Storm Desmond swept through. With so much damage to put right across such a huge area, a lag in the time it takes to initiate repairs is inevitable. But in the village of

Burneside, the bridge was surveyed and kept in use, reduced to a single lane. More recently, months of heavy rain has eaten away at the supports, and it has now been condemned. How much longer do we have to wait, and how many times will these scenarios play out? In the north Cumbrian town of Cockermouth, after the devastating floods of 2009, when the River Calder burst its banks and ran down the high street at the level of upper story windows, the sop to comfort the locals was talk of a once in a lifetime event. In the intervening years, two more extreme flood episodes have played out in that community, including during Storm Desmond. In the village of Staveley, a few miles upstream from Burneside, the village was literally divided that day by the collapse of the bridge in the middle of the main street, and the community was told that it would be two years before repairs could begin. But through sustained campaigning by local businesses, who, tired of waiting, and tired of the downturn in takings, planned to bring in their own bridge designers and builders—and to send the bill to the council. Then, at last, the county council agreed to bring forward the repairs; the bridge opened again last May, seventeen months after the storm.

∞

In July 2017, UNESCO granted the Lake District World Heritage Status. The announcement was accompanied by euphoric applause. But not by all. Central to the bid was the idea that sheep farming has created a 'cultural landscape' across the Lake District, of such great value that it was imperative that this should be preserved. A sheep farmer had been employed as a consultant on the bid. But what else would we have expected that farmer-consultant to say? Sheep, you could say, had taken centre stage. Sheep farming has been an integral part of the landscape here in The Lake District for centuries, and the Herdwicks, Swaledales and Rough Fell breeds live out all year round, grazing up to the mountain summits. They are *hefted*—having the ability to 'know' their place and how far to stray, or not. Farmers have commoner's rights to graze their herds over the open fells, even where ownership of that land is ascribed elsewhere.

The UNESCO descriptor of the Lake District tells us; *The stone-walled fields and rugged farm buildings in their spectacular natural backdrop, form an harmonious beauty that has attracted visitors from the 18th century onwards.* It goes on to say that from that time, Romantic engagement led to *a deeper and more balanced appreciation of the significance of landscape, local society and place,* and that in turn this led to the development of modern conservation movements—indeed to the founding of The National Trust. In the era in which these new ideas were developing, the relationship between humans and landscape began to be re-focussed, becoming a relationship built on emotional engagement, on the value that landscape has *for inspiring and restoring the human spirit; and the universal value of scenic and cultural landscapes, which transcends traditional property rights.*

But is it appropriate that those same ideals remain unaltered, unquestioned?

In the original bid document it states, (although this is not boasted about, hidden as it is in the middle of a vast document,) that our uplands are in poor condition. The bid writers tell you that trees have been cleared from the uplands since early man began to come in from the cold, to settle and build and farm, and therefore, the assumption is, we are not to blame for the loss of trees and scrub and therefore bio-diversity. But remember those early pastoralists, and how all they had at their disposal was the simplest of tools? And that hand axes were not used for the felling of trees? Let us be clear that the most significant amount of damage to the uplands of the Lake District came from the implementation of post-World War ll farming subsidies, which saw sheep numbers increase exponentially. Although sheep numbers have since reduced again, we know that their continuing presence in the wild landscape prevents regeneration—along with red deer. We know too that the uplands of Britain are the most deforested of all Europe. We know that overgrazing has brought with it the widespread loss of wildflowers and brambles and saplings, the invertebrates, the moths and butterflies, the birds and small mammals. (Wolves even, though as yet, that is a conversation too far.) And unless we begin to take seriously the strategic planting of new tree cover, what remains across most of the

Lake District, is a dereliction of trees and a paucity of wildlife. I should declare here that I am not suggesting the wholescale abolition of sheep farming in the Lake District; keep sheep by all means, but make much more space for trees.

I was brought up amongst farming people, and had close friends who farmed sheep, and some of those people were like family to me. Sheep farmers are some of the hardiest folk you are likely to meet. They work hard, and live and work in hard terrain. They are in tune with their way of life, and of the life cycle of the animals they keep. But is this enough? Now?

Who knows how that other elephant in the room will play out—the effects that Brexit will have on upland farming, or upon any farming in the UK for that matter, where income is dependent upon subsidies. And let us be clear that without the current level of subsidies, hill farming is *not* a viable way to make a living. In the light of this, and in the understanding that we live in a place where our shifting climate has the power to bring lives to a shuddering halt, to bring mountainsides tumbling down, isolating town from town, families from their homes, businesses from employees and to sweep away and drown cattle in their dozens, there are a handful of questions that we would do well to make central to our collective thinking, here in the north of England.

What purposes should landscape perform? Is it really sufficient that landscape should be considered as having a purely aesthetic function, like the viewing stations those Victorians created to look at waterfalls?

And that *idea* of *an harmonious landscape,* that outmoded, outdated Victorian idea, couched in arcane language, does it still apply? Does this have any relevance in this place, and at this time? (Yes, but with limitations.) Whose aesthetic is the most fit for purpose – the farmer's, or the forester's or the ecologists, or for that matter the two thousand families who lost their homes on 5th December 2016 in Kendal alone, and many of whom were unable to return for twelve months or more? Is it viable for us to continue looking out for the few, the people whose families have farmed here for centuries and some of whom intend to hold onto the land, to *preserve* it, and a single way of using it, like a sparrow hawk holds onto its prey, pressing on and on until the heart is stopped, and the life goes out? Or is time overdue to begin implementing change on a landscape scale that supports a more useful set of results, especially for communities downstream?

And without being possessed of a rich dimension and variety of wildlife, isn't landscape merely background?

Perhaps, like Edward Acland, we should all pay more attention. Wordsworth once met a man close to his home in the village of Grasmere, and asked him a question, the relevance of which has become more relevant than ever; *how is it that you live, and what is it that you do?* To protect our homes and businesses here in the land of mountains and mountains of rain, it is the planting of millions of trees that should now take centre stage. Not sheep; not any more. We need to think about our towns and their inhabitants as well as our rural landscapes and residents, and to do this, we need to think about rivers, and about what our rivers need in order to function as best they can. (And if they had a voice, what I know is that here in the Lake District, those rivers would speak about trees.) *Then* I will be happy to engage in conversations about *cultural landscapes*, but not before.

It is no longer possible to merely think about our rivers and their valleys as places to escape to, from where to consider the landscape in isolation, as a discreet presence that is somehow disconnected from us; that we gaze upon, remote and removed. We have the hard evidence of the way trees impact positively upon rivers. We know that they slow the flow by absorbing more rainwater than you or I could usefully imagine, and were they here in sufficient numbers, they would help to significantly slow down the next biblical flood from the three rivers of the Mint, the Sprint and the Kent, and from all the other rivers, when the next storm comes to call.

UNDER THE SHADE OF A STRINGYBARK

Margi Prideaux

There is a music to the river, for those who pause to listen.

In the midst of this hot dry land, precious water flows where I lie. This stream, scarcely more than a creek here, will eventually flow into the Western River. It is an untamed space that performs a wild opus.

I wonder who has composed the sprawling music it plays. Is it one composer or a grand collaboration?

Minutes ago, I walked through a swaying sea of grasses, baked and glowing by a sun amplified in the vast, brittle blue Australian sky. After a day working in its full glare, it felt like I was walking through a roaring campfire. My arms were scorched, and my body clamoured to lower a racing temperature. My heat-scalded head thumped with each step, but I could hear the inviting, buffeting rhythm of hot dry air drumming against moisture.

Nearing the creek line, the lure of deep shade from towering trees was only steps away. The buzz and hum of insects flirting with grasses gave way to a different choir of chirps and craws, twirls and twills. A distant banshee call echoed across the treetops, *'Scwreee-ahhh, scwreee-ahhh, scwreee, scwreee, scwreee-ahhh'*. Achingly beautiful, the ghostly timbre of the glossy black cockatoo's hymn resonates in harmony with the souls of this ancient land.

Wet shade. Big trees. Precious elements in a parched dry landscape. They exist, only, because of water.

Water that is music.

I cherish these moments, in the presence of these ancient, stringybark trees and the water at their feet. They stand as a family, branches embracing each other with care and grace. Roots anchored deep in the soil of the creek, sustained in the summer by a network of underground streams. Their torsos, coated in rich hues of silver, cream, and brown, unwrap in places. Where the bark lifts from the trunk, it is fringed with threads—*stringy*bark. Russet sap paints accents here and there, flowing through the cracks and gaps of the tree's weave. Juvenile branches celebrate life with luminescent splashes of lime green leaves on deep red stems. The canopy of this grand family towers as high as four London buses, end to end. The dark green adult leaves group together, casting deep shade. In other parts of Australia, these same species reach twice this height. Always, they stand in the company of water.

Here in the shade, the atmosphere is more softly focused than the open golden field not more than thirty steps away. In this place a cool fantasia plays. In the field, the heat of the day is so intense the air above the grasses blurs.

In a few weeks, the canopy above my head will laugh with a million flowers, and just as many wild bees will converge on the small white bursts of threads, surrounding tiny disks of rich nectar. Once the ceremony of the bees has woven its magic, the flowers will form petite fruits the shape of wine glasses, before ripening into seed pods, better known in Australia as 'gum nuts'.

Oblivious to the long history and understanding of this tree held by indigenous peoples, this species of stringybark were the first *Eucalyptus* species discovered and published by European explorers. Collected in 1777 by botanist David Nelson, it was the species used by Charles Louis L'Héritier de Brutelle in 1788 as the type species for the new *Eucalyptus* genus. He named these stringybarks *oblique,* from the Latin '*obliquus*' referring to the base of the leaves that are larger on one side than the other. There is little recognition of music in that title. I am sure, had L'Héritier passed an afternoon under their branches—had he listened to the opus the trees and water perform—he would have given them a lyrical name.

Now, at the height of summer, the creek appears still, but this is a deception. Running water is naturally rare in this landscape, and rarer still in the last five decades because my species has cleared and dammed much of the terrain, annihilating many creeks and streams, and their music. I imagine the remaining creeks trying to hide from view, lest someone comes to destroy their songs, but these creeks are too joyful to hide. Their masquerade is given-away by flute-notes as the water dances around the stringybark trunks and roots. On hot, dry days, everything that can move makes its way towards them to survive the heat, enjoy their cheerful company, and wait for nightfall. For a moment the breeze ebbs, the birds fall silent, and except my breath, a trickle is the only sound.

Stretching along the length of my favourite log that lies half submerged in the water, I reach down to float my hand in the flowing stream. My blood cools and my fingers tingle. The water is soft, like velvet, and gently tugs my hand. A ripple of peace flows up my arm, and the water hums it's melody.

This creek begins on our farm, rainfall collecting in the large fields to the west, pooling in rivulets, and sinking deep into the soil and underground streams that eventually make their way to this point. Below ground, it's as deep as the trees are tall and as dark as storm clouds. Above ground, it's shallow and clear as tea-coloured glass.

Where the shade from the stringybarks meets the field, the bright yellow baubles of wattle flowers bob in the breeze, keeping time with a rhythm my ears cannot hear. Wattle roots cling to the edge of the damp soil, their branches thrust out into the brightness of the sun. Purple thistle blossoms sit below the splashes of yellow.

Pushing their way to the fore, bracken cloaks the ground in a pillowed blanket of miniature Christmas trees along slender stems. Small clumps of fish-bone water ferns hug the water's edge, separated by the more abundant but no less beautiful coral ferns, their leaves lines of small green swords standing in formation along russet shoots. Pale rushes, adorned with straw-coloured flower heads, find space here and there. Other grasses twine between the trunks, ferns and rocks, some with early purple flower heads ripening to shining cream, others morphing between pale green and silver-white.

A frog peeps from behind a frond hanging into the water. Its rotund eyes blink lazily, then it submerges and with a powerful push shuttles itself across the creek bed, towards tall sedges. Tipping and bobbing, a painted lady butterfly, dances into view. A frenzy of orange, black and white, it lands for a moment on a seed-head waving to and fro as a gentle breeze moves its stage.

A rustle to my right.

I become conscious of another large presence.

I have never understood how mammals seem to be aware of each other, but even before they come into view, I know there is warm blood approaching. Flattening myself further against my log, I turn my head to peek between tufts of swaying grasses. The chocolate brown arch of a kangaroo's back advances.

Two ears emerge. Darker than the animal's body, the tips highlighted by iridescent bronze as he moves through the dappled light. Ears twitch, his head shakes. He turns to regard me. I slow my breath, and remain still as I can, my hand still trailing in the water. I've learnt that the smallest movement sends these beautiful beings away.

He glides into full view, slowly rising upright by taking his weight on a heavily muscled tail. He stamps his gaze on me. Although he signals no violence or threat, his broad muscled frame pulses with power. He's no youngster. His chest is etched with thick, cut muscles and his thighs are as wide as drums. Scars cross his shoulder and side, evidence of fights with other bucks. Yet, doe-eyes, like dark pools, above a downy black muzzle, watch me watching him. He decides I am to be trusted—for the moment.

Delight swells inside me. To be accepted by the wild is thrilling.

He drops to his forelegs and begins slowly grazing the grasses below his feet, eyes closing in peaceful study. His chewing, adds a new layer of percussion to the creek's music. His body becomes a pendulum rocking from his hind legs, onto his tail and forelegs, then his hind legs again. With rolling locomotion, he ambles forward to the next delicious morsel.

After a minute or two of companionable communion, the kangaroo stops, twitches his ears, and gazes beyond me. I slowly turn my head, then my body on the giant log to look at the creek behind.

I hold my breath for a moment. The gentle munching of grass resumes.

Good. I haven't disturbed him.

Above, a breeze excites the branches that now bob and sway, with a rustle like brushing cymbals, creating spaces where shafts of light break through the canopy. As if the trees intend it, the patch of brilliance illuminates a dragonfly, its wings tiny stained glass windows.

Beyond, is a cluster of thick bracken, ferns and grasses so thick that the small space looks like a pond surrounded by solid ground. I know better. A year ago I followed the creek, weaving my way through the dense vegetation, clambering over huge branches and under trunks dipped low, to where the stream snaked in a sharp left then right bend. This jive created a deep hole, so dark I couldn't see the bottom. Now I can hear the water flow through the pool, adding a deeper resonance to the opus.

I've toyed with swimming in that rare pool of deep water, when the Australian summer days reach their baking worst, but I always dismiss the allure. Many other beings will be there too. I'd gladly slide into the water with frogs and fish. Perhaps even the occasional goanna, but this is tiger snake country, and while we have developed a happy equilibrium with these lethally venomous snakes on our farmland, we have not established any ground-rules for sharing a small and inviting pond.

Tiger snakes are strong swimmers, their heavily muscled bodies creating rhythmic ripples across the surface. It's a magnificent sight. With bodies longer than my arm-span, they often doze in the water and are too easily mistaken for a submerged branch or tree root.

A bite from a snake, rudely awoken from slumber, followed by the clamour to get out of the pool, the stumble back through the dense bush, and the sprint across the wide field to call for medical help would probably end my days on this Earth. So, I content myself with an hour or two, by myself, lying face down on the bank, perched on my elbows while I gaze into the depths of the pool studying life underwater. Not today though. I am enjoying the presence of the buck nearby too much to break the peace between us.

I remain on my log, hand still in the water, a pleasant chill rising up my arm.

I am absorbed in a performance of a gentle opus.

Rhapsody.

I turn to observe the buck again, and contemplate the journey of this creek. Fallen logs and branches, twice the width of wine barrels lay across and around the stream as if the giant trees are weaving a tapestry at their feet. The log where I now lie is so wide that my arms only reach halfway around it. Over the years, part of its bulk has sunken into the cool, moist soil. The bark is still stringy, and a whole community of insects have colonised this space, creating an urban oasis for their communion. Their tiny clicks and buzzes, barely audible, are there nonetheless. Pea green moss hugs the earth in the areas of deep shade. Stringybark leaves scatter across the ground, adding green and bronze, ochre and cream to the tapestry of roots and fallen limbs created by the trees. Music of colour and form.

From here, the creek flows into the South Branch of the Western River. As the water winds its way across the landscape, it moves from our farm through a towering plantation of Tasmanian Blue Gums; massive stands of trees that will eventually be harvested to make paper. Then it flows briefly through another farm before it weaves north into bushland untouched by time.

As it meanders along, many other creeks feed its fantasia, the hills become steeper and the valleys deeper. Close to the coastline, it meets what is called the Western and Eastern Branches and falls into its final valley, where the river becomes wide and slow, the crescendo embracing the sea.

At this coastal end, the river has created a place of breathtaking beauty, flowing into a wetland nestled at the base of two perilously steep hills. Standing there it's as if the world around shuttled vertical and forgot to take the wetland with it. On either side, the hills rise 100 metres, too steep to climb for anyone but billy goats. Although sheep have been grazing these hills for decades, persistent woody plants still grip the soil, creating a patchwork of texture.

The river mixes with the salt of the ocean in an estuary flanked on one side by a pearl white beach and on the other by weathered ironstone rocks, etched and carved into honeycomb. As the hills themselves round to meet the deep blue water, their faces become sheer cliffs anchored beneath the waves. They stand as sentinels either side of the small bay. At that end, there are only two ways to commune with this river; by a single dirt road that weaves its way into the valley, or by boat arriving into the small bay.

More than a century ago, naturalists did just that.

Historic photos show tenacious scientists posing on the beach as their crates, barrels, and equipment were rowed ashore and stacked in the sand. The men stand proudly in their heavy woollen clothing. Ties tied around their necks. Walking sticks confidently held with one hand, while the other hand grips the front of their coats. The women stand just as tall and proud in their Victorian hats, ornate cotton shirts buttoned high under their chins, and heavy, ankle-length woollen skirts dragged down at the hems by the sand. They came to this place to collect plant and animal specimens for the South Australia natural history museum. What a relief it must have been to discover plentiful freshwater, only to blink with dread at the enormity of the hills they had to climb.

In our present time, it's easy to mistake the downhill path of the river as having come through farming country. There are small pockets of cleared land it has performed to but, this is, for the most part, still a wild river with forests untouched by modern man. Great sections, especially the Western Branch, have likely not felt the fingers of more than a dozen human's stroke its waters since Aboriginal communities lived here more than two thousand years ago. Between that bay and our farm, the river flows through vegetation so thick, and hills so steep, with access mostly through privately owned land, that no-one goes there. No-one hears the river's symphony.

The rhythmic munching from the buck nearby abruptly stops. My companion stands from his meal, inhales deeply with kangaroo contentment, and springs towards the creek. It's amazing to watch this change from the rocking locomotion to a delicate bounce, as if a balloon has been gently pushed forward, lighter than air. A few hops and he stoops his head low to drink in the bronze-tinged water.

A distant '*scwreee-ahhh, scwreee-ahhh, scwreee-ahhh*' echoes again. In reply, a group of rainbow lorikeets land in the canopy above, their chorus a cacophony of staccato screeches, amplified by raucous flashes of colours. Small living rainbows, twisting and twirling, and then they are gone.

Sipping and exhaling, the buck creates ripples that spread across the creek to the bank on the other side. Almost imperceptibly, there is a change in the tone of the river's song. The buck has become part of the lyrical language.

I gaze into the water as the creek continues the recital.

It's a masterpiece created by the wind, falling leaves, snakes winding through reeds, frogs gliding underwater, lorikeets, cockatoos, and kangaroos stooping to drink. The river performs this fugue through the landscape to the sea, adding to its masterful arrangement as it flows.

Life has composed the music of this river, under the shade of stringybark trees.

TROPICAL UPLAND RIVERS

Tropical and Subtropical Upland River ecoregions are dominated and defined by low-latitude non-floodplain rivers, including headwater drainages and tributaries of large river systems. These rivers are characterized by moderate gradients without cyclically flooded, fringing floodplains.

WILDER RIVERS—FRENCH AMAZONIA

Donna Mulvenna

Between gaps in the overhead branches, a rose-pink sky turned powder-blue. Wispy white clouds hinted at a fine day, but December was the start of the wet season in French Guiana, and there would be rain; not a brief drenching here and there, but a sustained wetness that made my home smell like jaguar's breath.

My partner, Frank lowered our sprint canoe from the village's timber jetty into the creek. A pungent odour of decomposing mangroves filled the air as I contemplated the tea-coloured water. Frank shook his head, his signal for, 'No time to swim, let's paddle.' Grinning, I hugged a smooth wooden pylon and slithered into the water. For twenty strokes, I swam hard against the current, then flipped onto my back, and with slow, turbine strokes floated to the jetty. Frank grasped my outstretched hand, hoisting my dangling feet clear of mud deep enough to swallow a zebu. Water streamed from my body, taking with it the stress and busyness of life.

Along the creek bank, *Pachira* trees burst into riotous yellow and scarlet blossom. Behind, an emerald green jungle pulsated with animal sounds, each creature it seemed, desperate for their buzzes, caws and chirps to be heard above all else. On the shoreline, a mangrove rail startled from her nest. She peered in our direction, strutted like a high-stepping chicken, and probed the mud with her long curved beak. Nearby, a threatened shoal of big-eyed fish zigzagged away. The bird protested with a clattering *kek-kek-kek.*

Boasting an impressive bird list of over 700, French Guiana, one of the world's last tracts of original, undisturbed tropical rainforest, is home to residents that stay all year long, to breeding birds that spend a good part of the growing season, to migrants who pass through with the seasons, to wintering birds who prefer the tropics to colder northern conditions.

Until I visited the *French* Amazon, I hadn't recognised how the wilderness would reshape my priorities, teach me about myself, and whet my appetite for more. It was the opposite of my life in Australia, where I existed like a circus performer spinning plates, too focused on impressions and outcomes to relax. My hectic lifestyle, and the stress I was under, clouded my brain so I didn't appreciate the calm green shades of nature or the cool blue of the sea.

On the river, at dawn, life flowed at a calmer pace.

We kneeled in the canoe, a seven-metre-long streak of fluorescent green and gold, and pushed off. The canoe sliced through the water like a warm knife through butter. It was a very different craft to the territory's traditional pirogue, a dugout carved from a single log and as sturdy as a sea cow.

'I hope we find a waterfall today,' I said, recalling a conversation with our neighbour. Unlike my Australian neighbours who knew only the stretch of water in front of their canal-side homes, Guianese villagers had a clear and detailed knowledge of the river, several days paddling up and down.

Ahead, three young children paddled a pirogue. The eldest child held a long *takari* pole and steered the boat with the same enthusiasm a city child peddles a three-wheeled cart along the sidewalk. The second child caught fish using a home-made rod, catching lunch rather than carrying a sandwich in a clip lock plastic bag. Finally, a little girl of around five, laughed as she pointed to a weaverbird, a yellow-rumped cacique that clung to the side of a sock-shaped nest. Unprotected from the elements, they wore no sun hats or streaks of sunblock on their glowing faces, nor life jackets to buoy their tanned bodies. The young girl spotted us first. She whispered to the second child who tapped the boy holding the *takari*. All three faced us, and like fawns transfixed by car headlights they froze, their alert eyes watching us from behind braids adorned with red and white beads.

We stopped paddling to float alongside them. 'You look strong,' said Frank. 'How about a race?'

Giddy with excitement, the tallest boy leaped into position, the boat's bow bouncing to life. The two younger children slid to opposite sides of a wooden bench, their builds so slight the pirogue hardly flinched. They held their timber paddles aloft and stared straight ahead.

Against a backdrop of singing songbirds, Frank called, 'Hold it steady. Wait. Three, two, one... Go!'

Shrieks rang out as six slender arms flailed through the air like windmills. The pirogue grudgingly inched forward. With all their might the children paddled, their silhouettes turning dark green in the shadows of overhanging branches, and pale green in the light. After the length of a cricket pitch, with tired arms and heaving chests, they accepted the folly of racing a heavy timber boat and stopped. The eldest boy waved his paddle in the air and called, '*Monsieur*, only today you win.'

Frank waved back. 'Yes, you had us worried for a while.'

The children giggled.

Beyond an enclave of shiny black rocks, fresh water from the Tumak Humak Mountains collided with salt water from the Atlantic to form a wide, fast-flowing river. A high escarpment afforded a natural defence from the wind, but still turbulent whirlpools swirled around the canoe. Deep in concentration we paddled in unison—heads down, arms up, strong backs, breathe, until we shot between the piers of a rusted iron bridge and reached calmer water. In the small sheltered bay, a startled fisherman glared at us unsmiling. Had we frightened off his piranhas?

People often asked about the river's hazards. We stressed that Guianese piranhas were the vegetarian kind, black caimans were shy, and anacondas were misrepresented, but still friends regarded us dubiously. Even when we assured them a racing canoe would not be an ideal choice for infested waters, they grinned back as if waiting for a punch line.

A yellow pirogue motored past, its tattered blue tarpaulin snapping the air like a cracking whip, and its tired engine dinging in time to chirping crickets. My gaze settled beyond the pirogue, at a medley of tree roots, undergrowth and thick alligator weed. I hoped to see a crab dog or even better, the cutest animal in the Amazon resembling a seal cub crossed with a sweet potato—the manatee. Reaching a weight of 800kg, manatees are South America's largest mammals, feasting daily on up to 50kg of mangrove seedlings or moucou-moucou, the wide, heart-shaped leaves of Arum plants.

Chiming laughter filtered through the mangroves, its jubilant nature propelling us around the next bend at speed. On a raised section of riverbank, a large family leaned over the crooked railing of an open, weather-beaten *carbet*. A voice boomed from the back.

'A giant anaconda lives here!'

'There are snakes everywhere,' called Frank. The voice guffawed before sinking back into the curve of its hammock.

Three boys shouted. '*Allez plus vite*, Go faster.' A group of teenaged girls hung freshly scrubbed laundry on tree branches, and two middle-aged women dressed in brightly-coloured kangas washed crockery from a submerged step. An elderly man nursing a shotgun squatted on the shore, a skinny boy dangled from a palm tree, and a group of young girls with water glistening from their dark skin like sequins, somersaulted from the balcony into the water. River spray spattered across the surface, blue, turquoise and green droplets catching the sun like peacock feathers. Children with carefree natures living colourful lives, in a scene as lush as any image from the Jungle book, but as unpredictable as the Bermuda triangle.

'*Bonjour messieurs dames*,' called a group of fishermen on the bank. 'Stop and talk to us.'

For all the years we paddled along Australian rivers, we had never been invited to stop and chat. Most times we paddled by unnoticed, the housing estates facing away from rivers so they could overlook busy roads that led to airports, cities and shops. We pushed our canoe onto a small sandy beach.

'*Bonjour*,' called Frank, 'what have you caught?'

Two fishermen held up an armoured catfish, almost as big as the one we watched a villager tie to a pole, and carry home over his shoulder, its tail dragging on the ground. With over 500 members of catfish in the

Amazon this was one of the biggest, but the best-eating were reputedly those which gave off a rich, red sauce when boiled—just like ketchup.

Two young boys, about six or seven, kicked a football. Judging from the soles of their feet, they always played barefoot. They weren't vocal, but their game was ferocious. In a final foot tussle, a boy kicked the ball to Frank who charged towards it with flared nostrils, booting it between two driftwood goal posts. Within seconds, a dozen children stampeded from the forest. Unsure of which way to run, to the canoe or the football, they stopped mid-way. Holding his hands high in defeat, Frank tossed the ball back to the boys and headed for the canoe. One group of children trotted behind, the other, a more daring group sprinted ahead, dropping to their knees in front of him, and air paddling with sticks.

A teenaged boy curled his arm around the waist of a boy who stared at his own feet, and whispered in his ear. With a radiant smile, and scratching his belly, the shy boy approached Frank and asked, '*Excusez-moi, monsieur,* may we try?'

Frank rested his chin in the palm of his hand and looked thoughtful. Every child stared, silent and wide-eyed, until the peace was shattered by a boy sprinting and hollering from the jungle. '*Attends moi monsieur,* wait for me!'

As if the action had broken a curse, Frank peered into each of the dark eyes drilling into his, and announced, '*Bien sûr,* certainly!'

The older children punched the air and high-fived. The little ones ran in circles. Frank's face crinkled. He had so much life in his eyes, yet he was always calm and patient with children. I didn't know whether he was born that way or had mellowed after decades of paddling.

When the children calmed down, they formed an orderly queue, with no coaxing. The girls swimming in front of the carbet stopped splashing. Realising canoe rides were taking place, they leapt from the water yelling, '*Nous arrivons*, we're coming!'

My gaze settled on the tallest boy. 'Are you all good swimmers?'

'*Oui, madame*, we swim like fish.'

Each child agreed, including an adolescent girl who strode from the beach carrying what I hoped was a legless lizard and not a snake. When she offered me the reptile, I jumped back and shook my head. She grinned showing a perfect set of white teeth. Her black hair had been separated into a dozen or more locks, each captured at the tip by a clear bead which rattled when she nodded. Other children demonstrated their doggy paddle skills.

My eyes narrowed. Frank winked and signalled for me to wade into the river.

The first boy tried desperately to stay in the canoe. He waved his paddle overhead, wobbling like an unsteady gymnast during beam practice. When he fell, the shock of hitting the water and the speed at which it happened, combined with a throat full of water, rendered him helpless. I rushed forwards to pluck him from the river, which had already taught me it was as fierce and unpredictable as any rip in the Pacific. Falling from the canoe early one morning, the current picked me up and carried me towards the sea like an inflatable pool toy. A strong swimmer, I proved no match for a current renowned for dumping up to two thousand, average-sized swimming pools worth of water into the Atlantic, every second.

The next boy listened to Frank's instructions more intently. '*Oui, monsieur*,' he said, not stopping to take a breath, 'I understand.' His eyes jerked from Frank to the canoe.

Frank kneeled behind the boy and together they pushed off. I held my breath as the lad twisted mid-air and buckled over.

He stayed in.

'Well done,' said Frank, with sincerity. 'Now relax and breathe.' The boy's back straightened and he looked ahead, his eyes unblinking. He submerged the blade to advance the boat a few metres. With renewed confidence, he took a stronger stroke, then another, his body tilting to one side until he reached the point of no return and toppled into the water. In a Mexican wave, the children squatting on the bank rose from the ground and roared with laughter. Then, realising it was their chance, they surged forwards pleading for it to be their turn as if their young lives absolutely depended on it.

After every child had kneeled in the canoe, we waved goodbye.

'*Merci beaucoup, monsieur. Merci beaucoup, madame,*' the children said, before darting barefoot and laughing back into the rainforest. My heart ached a little when they had gone. This riverside community had welcomed us, despite us being foreigners with a sordid history of pillaging their home.

Back on the river, two jet skis zoomed past, doubling back and churning up the water. 'Hoons!' I said out loud, but then felt sorry because their noisy machines robbed them of wildlife sightings, the real thrill of the river. Overhead, storm clouds gathered, and the temperature dipped. My fingers curled tightly around the paddle, and Frank, the engine in the rear of the canoe, shifted to high gear.

The race against the rain was on.

For every metre gained, ten raindrops bounced off the canoe's deck. To our right, the space between the river and sky blurred to tin-cup grey. I couldn't see the rain, but I could smell the earthy scent of it as it hammered onto rock and soil. It was gaining on us.

'To the *matouchi* tree,' Frank yelled, when the deluge blasted from the rainforest and struck us in diagonal sheets.

With squinted eyes, I tucked my chin to my chest. Water poured from my cap, streaming from my nose. My heart pumped just enough oxygen for the sprint. Against the bank, I grabbed an overhanging branch to steady myself. Hundreds of almond-sized raindrops dumped on me. I couldn't have been any wetter if I'd dived in. Lightning ripped through the sky, a blinding incandescence that turned the darkened river hot silver.

Part of me wanted to shout out, knowing that except for Frank, there wasn't another soul to hear me or cast doubt upon my sanity. Instead, I smoothed away my goose bumps with one hand. 'It's remarkable,' I said, 'the force of it.'

Frank made no comment. There was no need for the air was ripe with mutual understanding.

Two emerald-coloured parrots streaked overhead, and a dozen red-legged crabs with bulging yellow eyes side-stepped along aerial roots. On the opposite bank, a flock of scarlet ibis roosted, their ruby-red shapes hanging like baubles from a juniper Christmas tree. Chilled and dripping, we were *all* plugged into Nature's swirling rhythm, being life instead of doing life.

When the sunlight bullied its way through the clouds, and lone raindrops could be heard plonking onto broad leaves, we pushed into the swollen river.

The air buzzed like overhead power lines.

A capybara rose from flattened grass.

A kingfisher executed a perfect splashless dive.

It was business as usual.

At a creek entrance concealed by a fallen tree amassing slimy vegetation, Frank asked, 'Are you tired?' His question was laced with unspent energy.

'No, I'm hot,' I answered, 'but nothing a swim wouldn't fix.' Raising my nose into the air, I asked, 'Can you hear that noise?'

'A waterfall?' Frank steered the canoe through a vertical screen of mangrove roots.

'Let's go drifting,' I suggested, patting myself on the back for my brilliant idea.

Drifting along Amazonian rivers felt the same as strolling through deep countryside. The constraints of the city fell away, leaving a remoteness and quietness that made the surroundings feel like mine. My body strained free from urban chains beneath trees as tall as church spires, my *sense* of superiority deflated under the shadows of large, fan-shaped leaves, and my senses were tantalised by the flicker of tamarin monkeys. But being able to observe the forest from its foundation was the *pièce de résistance*—deep leaf litter covering rich soil, red translucent fungi and animal tracks—all robust but fragile, in an isolated area people don't normally see.

I listened for birdsong, but the day had shifted to blazing; too hot for the small songbirds perched on branches like statuettes, open-beaked and gasping. The heavy air created a silence, one that souls can hear but ears cannot, when the river appeals to our basic human instinct. I opened my mouth to pledge my respect, and to acknowledge that on the river, the difference between right and wrong became clearer, when...

'*Growl. BARK*!'

Stunned, I couldn't decide whether to flee or fight, so my brain took the third option and froze. Only my eyeball twitched.

Seconds ticked by. Inwardly, I retraced our path to minutes before when a surprised capybara fled, kicking up a mighty spray of water. The Amazon's largest rodent and a favourite food of jungle cats, combined with no sign of human life for over an hour had to mean a jaguar.

I waited for an animal to plunge from the river into our boat. Nothing.

Spinning my head in an arc, I scanned the dark undergrowth for movement. Not a crackle.

A cloud shadow passed overhead.

'*SNORT!*' This time closer. My eyes strained through photons of dim light. A break in the surface. A chocolate-coloured head shot out. It had small, round ears and bulging eyes that never left me. It didn't look pleased.

'A giant otter,' said Frank. 'It's protecting its territory. Quick, paddle back.'

Years earlier, in a BBC documentary, I viewed a family of indestructible giant otters crush a fully grown caiman. A tingling sensation spread across my chest. In the wake of a small tsunami, I paddled back.

Satisfied, the otter dove.

We waited, the sound of anticipation deafening.

Swoosh. Further downstream the otter resurfaced. Dappled sunlight reflected off its whiskers and the dominant white patch on its neck. It gauged us with a blank, unalarmed aloofness. Then, in a flurry of movement, swished its broad tail and vanished.

Minutes ticked by. Nothing.

A cormorant sitting on the bank jerked its S-shaped neck, evidently agitated by our presence.

Drifting quietly, I willed my ears to hear snorting or high-pitched whistling. Eventually I detected a loud inhale, '*Uhhg*' followed by a soft exhale and '*ah,*' then silence, then '*Uhhg-ah.*' On the far bank, a romp of otters chirped, purred and chuckled. A large otter sunning itself spotted us the instant we saw it. Before I had time to form a single thought, it plunged into the water followed by a family who put every ounce of their energy into a dash for cover.

'Where did they go?' I asked.

'If those two kingfishers that u-turned are following them, I'd say that way.' Frank pointed to where the river bent around a long curve, the inside harbouring a small silty beach, the outside highly eroded.

'Let's follow,' I suggested.

'I think they've had enough disruption for one day,' said Frank.

'You're right.' I said, mentally smacking myself on the forehead for being as clueless as those who venture to near wildlife to take selfies.

I tilted my head to the side. 'I hear the waterfall.'

The narrow creek meandered, then like an anaconda having swallowed a peccary, it swelled into a large waterhole. On the rocky banks, green palms, ruby-red bromeliads, and yellow lichens gathered like a Jackson Pollock painting. A blue morpho butterfly fluttered past, its radiance turning the fairy tale scene more lifelike.

Curiously, a red fuel drum bobbed towards us. Knowing something was amiss we paddled on. A fallen tree blocked our way, forcing us to make a sharp right turn to avoid being snagged by splintered timber. On the other side, we coasted into an enormous pile of rubbish.

On the river bank, a make-shift shelter built by lashing polyester cord between trees and erecting a tarpaulin, sagged to the ground.

'It's an abandoned gold mine.' Irritation flared in Frank's voice.

The ramshackle settlement where illegal miners had lived and worked, rendered a large area of the forest bare of ferns, trees and flowers. Nature diligently worked towards restoring harmony, but a mountain of manmade rubbish remained: broken baby strollers, smashed toys and soiled clothes. We stepped over shattered glass and rubber tyres, and crunched over metres of black, agricultural-grade plastic. Dented jerricans littered the ground alongside threaded nylon rice sacks and a battered deep freezer. Polystyrene food containers, shopping bags and engine parts clogged a small stream.

A string of expletives swarmed in my mind.

The miners had chosen to live in these harsh conditions, but what about their children? Were they distraught when forced to leave their toys? What had prompted this small destructive workforce to cross into French Guiana and treat its beautiful, pristine, natural environment as a rubbish tip? Were the miners so accustomed to wild beauty they had become immune to it, or had poverty left them little choice? Regardless, for a few flecks of gold, the rainforest would need hundreds of years to recover; a fallout consumers standing on red carpets in jewellery stores never see.

Frank gathered the rubbish, setting one pile of burnable items aside, another pile to collect later. With the unprecedented rate of habitat destruction throughout other parts of the Amazon and the world, French Guiana may become the last example of undisturbed rainforest on earth. Yet, illegal mining persists in an anarchic manner, with high concentrations of the mercury used to recover fine gold particles from sediments poisoning the rivers, the wildlife and a native population subsisting on a diet primarily of fish.

Eager to distance ourselves from this blatant reality, we paddled away with determined strokes. A brooding silence replaced my earlier happiness as I contemplated the cost of living in my *civilised* world.

Amid my chaotic thoughts, the powerful three-note birdsong of a screaming Piha cut across the landscape. Its shrill *qui* paused momentarily before erupting into a loud *qui-yo* that abruptly vanished back into the forest.

Sunlight warmed my face.

Two toucans with short, stout bodies flew overhead, their wings beating at breakneck speed as if to hold up their oversized yellow-orange beaks.

I dipped my hand into the river, the beauty of everything overwhelming me. I withdrew my hand as a wiser woman, the river's essence urging me to build a reciprocal relationship with nature. As my mind cleared, my lips curved upwards. The children's smiling faces granted me hope, and the sighting of giant otters bestowed a sense of purpose.

TROPICAL FLOODPLAIN RIVERS

Tropical and Subtropical Floodplain River ecoregions are dominated by a single mid-latitude large river system, with a cyclically flooded, fringing floodplain. Like their temperate counterparts, these ecoregions may also contain wetland complexes composed of internal deltas, marshes, or swamps, associated with the main river system.

ON THE NEGRO RIVER

José Truda Palazzo, Jr.

I came to see the flood.

Once a year, following patterns established in the deep past before humankind disrupted the climate, an immense stretch of the Amazonian rainforest becomes literally a water garden. Beneath a show of lightning and thunder, the rain that falls continuously for weeks transforms thousands of rivers, streams, lakes and wetlands into a single aquatic realm.

As many Brazilians, I had never visited Amazonia. Looking at its location on a map, you don´t realize the distances to get to any of its main entry cities are truly gigantic, and those of us living south of the great forest pay a higher airfare to get there than to the Caribbean or Miami. But when close friends from the other side of the world—the Island of Yap in Micronesia—invited us on a two week private expedition from Manaus up the Negro river, it was too good an opportunity to miss. In May 2012, my wife and I, accompanied by my daughter

Lara, gazed over the great expanse of water which bordered the greenery near the Tropical Hotel of Manaus. Anchored at the water's edge was a bobbing *gaiola*—a typical two-story wooden boat used to carry passengers throughout the Brazilian Amazon.

The three of us would be the first Brazilian passengers ever to set foot on the *Tucano*, an Ecotourism-dedicated boat catering for International tourists who wish to see the unique ecosystems, wildlife and people of this legendary and endangered realm. 'Brazilians,' we are told by the Captain, 'with enough money to travel on the *Tucano* prefer to shop in Miami,' which helps to explain why Brazil's unique environmental heritage is going down the drain. Yet, here we were, thanks to the generosity of Bill and Patricia Acker, stepping onto a tiny speck of wood that would traverse the swollen river and navigate its raging currents.

The Negro, *black* in Portuguese, is a main artery of the vast river system that crisscrosses the Amazonian region and flows towards the Atlantic Ocean. Unlike the "true Amazon" or Solimões River, the Negro brings waters not from the relatively young terrains of the Andean slopes and Southern Amazon plains, but from the ancient, long-eroded highlands bordering Brazil and Venezuela. This region, known as the Guyana Shield, is rich in flat-topped *tepuis*, towering mountains carved out from hundreds of millions of years of erosion that surge vertically from the surrounding plains, and inspired Sir Arthur Conan Doyle to write *Lost World*.

Unlike the Solimões, which is brownish from the sediments it carries, the Negro is tinged with darker tones of humic acid—the product of decomposition of billions upon billions of leaves. When the rains wash the leaves into the flow, a unique and highly complex aquatic ecosystem is created. Downstream from Manaus, both mighty arteries fuse together continuing their long journey to the coast as a single, portentous Amazon River.

Relaxing in the *Tucano's* best cabin, the one perched high behind the wheelhouse, jungle life played out before our eyes. The boat chugged away from Manaus, clinging to jungle-fringed river banks where the river narrowed, surged through white-capped waves where the main channel widened, and navigated around temporary or permanent islands. Apart from a few elevated terraces, framed at the riverside by the brick-red *barrancas* or eroded slopes of clay, every land surface was covered by water. The trees and shrubs on the flooded plains evolved to withstand wet feet for months, millions of animal species evolving with it. As the boat snaked through the narrow passages of the Anavilhanas, the largest riverine archipelago in the world and now a National Park, I realized we were looking at the forest canopy, which meant at least ten meters of forest was hidden by the dark waters below. It was difficult to fathom that, during the dry season, guides walked tourists along the sandy tracks on the river bed where we cruised over now.

How had these plant and animal species adapted to such a radical change in their environment? The answer is concealed behind the aeons that passed since the mighty Andes started to rise, blocking the way for South American rivers to flow west, which forced them to turn east through the boundless plains towards the Atlantic shores. Submerged trees adapted not only to withstand prolonged waterlogging of their roots and lower trunks, but "learned" to cooperate with new partners in a quest for survival. Fish species adapted to the seasonally flooded forests eagerly wait for the flood. Multi-shaped fish swim among a maze of trunks and branches and feast on fruit, dropped at an opportune time to meet their needs. Aquatic dispersers, the fish carry heavy seeds far from individual trees. Many of the seeds are big and heavy, but so are the fish species in the Negro.

Freshwater fishing is a thriving business and the main means of survival for many communities scattered throughout the region. River giants like the *pirarucu*, which can attain three meters and more than 200kg, once depleted, are now rebounding to sustainable numbers due to strict management programs. Tasty species such as *tambaqui* are farmed, and every evening on the *Tucano*, this fish and other exquisitely prepared Amazonian fish were served to us from the grill. In the grand salon of the main deck, dinner conversation often turned to how unregulated, unsustainable (and still heavily subsidized) fishing in the Amazon, and worldwide, was killing our shared oceans. Over daily meals of fresh fish, the Captain and his passengers marvelled at the Amazon's capacity to supply most of the world's fish protein, and then dismayed that aquatic vandalism, called industrial fishing, risked that because it wasn't more efficiently managed.

At breakfast each morning, *Tucano's* guides entranced us with tales of ecological interactions, food webs and adaptations orchestrated by plants and animals to survive and prosper. At dawn the following day, I set off eager to see rare orchids, exotic birds, and canopy-dwelling marsupials. Instead, most of what we saw was a wall of green. The dense, stories-high jungle makes it difficult for untrained eyes to see some of the world's most secretive animals, many capable of camouflage. Disembarking at a trail, we walked between root buttresses and dangling vines as silently as possible. Along the route, the guides pointed to moist leaf litter or a dry tree trunk, savouring the long seconds it took for us naive visitors to strain our eyes and see ... nothing. With more detailed pointing, we finally realized that the small brownish leaf was a forest frog, and the bump on a dead trunk was actually a large, but superbly camouflaged, nightjar or potoo.

My fellow passengers were mostly excited about animals, but I was enthralled by an unsung and rarely noted group of living beings: fungi. In different sizes and textures, either colourful or drab and often glowing in the dark, giving an otherworldly appearance to patches of dead wood either fallen or hanging from the trees, I examined their fruiting bodies (the visible parts of most fungi, as their "roots", which are the real permanent stuff, lay hiding in the soil, dead wood or leaf litter), and deliberated over the fundamental role they played in maintaining the richness and fertility of the forest. I ran my hand along a clump of fungi, its cheese-like flesh as thick as an elephant's ear. Without fungi, and other species that aid in breaking down the forest's debris, there would be no topsoil or rainforest at all. The fungi needed moisture to operate, thriving during each rainy season.

When not walking along riverside tracks, we traversed creeks and the river in dugout canoes. Branches usually many meters above ground level now scraped our heads. Each branch harboured a veritable hanging garden where vivid-green mosses, scarlet-red bromeliads and pristine-white orchids could make the best landscape artists envious of their compositions. Especially enamoured by delicate lemon orchards, I appreciated that bromeliads were the true queens, ecologically speaking, of canopy gardens. Their vase-like arrangement holds considerable amounts of water even during drier periods, providing a safe haven for small critters such as tiny crabs and frogs to breed there, and a cup from which arboreal-living animals drink. Their flowers and fruit feed birds and monkeys, and their fluffy seeds adorn many birds' nests. More elusive to the untrained eye, but inescapable to our guides, were the snakes and spiders, including fist-sized tarantulas, that hunkered down in the florets of the bromeliads.

Not all the flooded forest denizens lived in hiding. At dawn and dusk, we left our cabin to watch large flocks of raucous, colourful birds fly overhead, in their incessant search for food or shelter. After a few days of nature watching, two groups of river-crossing birds became easily distinguishable: toucans and macaws. Toucans often flew parallel to the riverbank amusing us with their awkward short downward glides after what seemed to be rather strenuous wing beating. With extended beaks and sporting a variety of showy colours, from jet-black, light blue and white to bright orange, depending on species, they settled in small groups atop cecropia trees in sections of relatively open canopy.

Macaws rarely settled by the river. Their passing overhead was evident by their raucous calls, giving ample warning to watch big groups cross the river in organized squadrons, their cross-like appearance from below embellished by bright blues, reds and yellows.

Toucans hunt among the flooded forest greenery for nestlings of other birds and a variety of fruit, while macaws often seek the mind-boggling variety of Amazonian palm trees for their hard-shelled nuts, which they easily break with beaks strong enough to make you regret extending your finger to a captive one.

Farther along the river, an eerie and mysterious noise became more frequent. One late afternoon on the *Tucano's* deck, as we admired the changing colours of the sky during the sunset right after a huge thunderstorm, Lara heard a deep *poof* coming from the starboard side of the boat. Intrigued, a group of us leaned over the rail. Gliding in the water, shearing the surface with their elegant lines, was a family of pink dolphins, one of the most celebrated—and unfortunately beleaguered—symbols of Amazonia.

Pink dolphins share their waters with another small cetacean, the tucuxi, smaller than the robust 2.5 meters and 150 Kg of its rosy-skinned cousin. Neither are afraid of humans, regularly sweeping by our boat in small groups. It appeared the tucuxis kept mostly to the open waterways, while the pink dolphins were not shy of entering flooded plains where their flexible bodies and revered echolocation skills located fish and crabs amongst a maze of roots, tree trunks, and fallen branches.

The dolphins kept us company all the way to the Jauaperi River, our northernmost reach into the hyleaea. There, on a rare shallow sandbank reaching almost to the surface, our hosts deployed foldable chairs and a beer cooler. The dip in riverine environs provided an insider's perspective and offered a welcome reprieve from the oppressive heat. A family of pink dolphins circled the sandbank for a long while, their loud *poofs* and surface antics, including the occasional jump out of the water, extracting expressions of amazement from our multinational group.

It was with a mixture of joy and sadness that I watched the dolphins. I knew what was happening to these graceful animals in the upper Amazonian basin:

they were being slaughtered for bait. A giant species of catfish, the *piracatinga*, attracts hefty prices on the regional market, and is fished using traps baited with rotten meat. Settlers illegally hunt the dolphins and illegally catch the fish, often trading it with Colombian drug cartels and returning to Brazil with cocaine. An estimated 2,000 dolphins are killed every year to serve this indecent, vicious traffic, which the Brazilian authorities have tried, but failed to quench. Combined with the fragmentation of the Amazonian basin by mega-dams built on several rivers the survival of both Amazonian dolphin species are threatened in this century. With their species on the verge of oblivion, I try hard to shake these thoughts from my head as other passengers take photographs of the dolphins' antics, but they refuse to go away. Being an environmental activist is inescapable; once you know the terrible truth about the state of our planet, it's a 24/7 burden. Spending time on the Amazon River renewed my strength to fight the seemingly unwinnable battles ahead. The genuine concern of the captain and the staff about sustainable fishing practices offered me hope, and the flooded plains and the mass of diversity within served as a reminder of all that's at stake.

On the Jauaperi River, our guides pointed out another branch of the mammalian family: monkeys. Living high above the rising waters, the Amazon harbours the highest rates of primate diversity in the world. Fearless troops of squirrel monkeys, their yellowish body and masked faces evident against dark green foliage, leaped from branch to branch ravaging ripe fruits. To see some of the shyer species we took to the canoes again, drifting near to riverbanks and ducking under drowned trees, silently looking and listening for signs of activity. One species, whose male guttural screams could be heard from three kilometres, lived in small family groups. When they spotted our canoes, they would enter into a bout of screaming, then accustomed to our presence continued about the business of eating leaves. More elusive was the Bearded Saki. The guides pointed out a single family munching on some green fruits, their faces prominent against greenery, but didn´t stay long. Perhaps their shyness was on account of settlers waging a relentless war against them, and any other creature they deem edible. Sales of illegal bush meat are placing another burden onto the Amazon's ecosystem. Combined with well-known environmental crimes of deforestation and mega-dam building, the extirpation of Amazonian wildlife by unsustainable, unregulated hunting is a major tragedy, which authorities alleging "social" reasons, fail to address. How much more socially equitable and environmentally sound it would be to help local communities develop nutritional alternatives—these might be aquaculture and low-impact small-scale agroforestry—reducing their dependency on hunting. I fear the concerns of the Amazonian people will not be heard until more decision-makers enter the forest and hear the agonizing cries of wildlife before the final bullet hits.

As the *Tucano* rolled downriver, I reflected on what the Amazonian rivers had taught me—not only at the surface of the Earth, but above and below. Brazilian hydrologists and meteorologists have proven the moisture captured by the Amazonian rainforest and recycled through a cloud belt, travels south all the way to the Brazilian south eastern State of São Paulo, where agriculture and urban dwellers suffer the effects of regular droughts caused by rampant deforestation. Affected citizens sound alarm bells, scientists and environmentalists rally and advise, and yet the politicians continue to ignore.

The other Amazonian basin is not airborne and fast-flowing as jet streams allow; deeply embedded in the rocks below the entire Amazonian region, lies the Hamza system, a 4km deep underground river that flows for some 6,000km towards the Atlantic, just like its surface brothers. Although it flows at a slower pace, 10 to 100 meters/year instead of the Amazon River's two meters per second, it verifies the Amazon region is an enormous mass of water, above and below our expectations.

On our final leg of the journey, the *Tucano* takes us to the Meeting of the Waters, the legendary place where the dark Negro and the light brownish Solimões waters meet. Whirlpools crash and collide until the densities finally melt into a single, portentous flow traveling side by side for miles towards the eastern horizon. As the boat chugs towards Manaus, it faces the ugly, alien silhouette of the sprawling urban enclave. A raft of plastic and other garbage floats past.

Will humanity as a whole understand the true value of Nature in time to prevent Amazonia from collapsing? As a collective, can we safeguard waters which nurture the forest, wildlife and people, and accrue benefits from its existence without denying it to future generations? Ultimately, the Amazon's fate depends on the individual attitudes of all of us. A change is surely needed, but it must come soon, because time, just as the Amazonian waters, flows too fast.

DEAFENED BY NATURE

I recently returned from a two week visit to the heart of
Manu National Park in southeastern Peru. Cocha Cashu
is the name of a small cluster of rustic buildings that
make up the Biological Research Station for which I
work. It is also the name of the oxbow lake on the shore
of which the Station nestles: *cocha* is the Quechua word
for lake and Cashu refers to its cashew nut shape.

Oxbows are formed—abandoned, really—as a river
pinches off its loops over time to follow a shorter,
straighter course. Their size is thus determined by the
parent river, with which they eventually have little or
no connection. Some oxbows become impenetrable
swamps, while others evolve into oases for wildlife.
Cocha Cashu is one such oasis. Though rubber tappers
and loggers navigated the nearby Manu River—the
lake's creator—a century ago, and students of tropical
ecology from far-flung countries have made Cashu their
home since 1969, the area surrounding the Station is as

wild and pristine as any you're likely to find anywhere in the modern world.

This realisation was forcibly impressed upon me each day, most strikingly through the medium of sound.

Cocha Cashu is an extremely noisy place.

For one thing, I have no need of an alarm clock at Cashu. Between 4:30 and 4:45 am, without fail, I'm borne to the surface of consciousness by the deep, husky roars of howler monkeys. I once described it to my family as the sound of a train rushing through a tunnel and I still can't think of a better simile. The first time I heard it, years ago and at close quarters, I was momentarily paralysed with fright, until my husband explained what it was. As their roars rise to an almost supernatural crescendo, and before subsiding into a series of sawing coughs, it seems impossible that such a tremendous noise can come from an animal's throat. A rude awakening though it may be, I can't think of a better way to start a new day.

By 5am I'm usually sitting cross-legged in the stern of a small, needle-shaped canoe, hollowed out of a single tree trunk. With my camera and binoculars at my feet and a crudely carved wooden paddle in my hands, I'm ready to explore the lake. Being an otter biologist, my aim is to find the resident family of giant otters and to observe them during their morning hunt. But, *en route*, I also take the opportunity to tune into the lives of other residents. As the boat slips away from the dock, the shadows of night slink into the forest and shy stirrings on the shoreline become an urgent scramble for food and mates. Cries of every description begin to ring across the lake.

On one such morning, at about 6:30am, I wrote down all the different sounds I could identify within a period of five minutes.

First to register were the monkeys: a forlorn hiccupping of dusky titis, disturbingly reminiscent of crying human babies, followed by the hysterical ululating of gangly, aptly named black spider monkeys. Howlers on one side of the oxbow again began their unearthly chorus and a group on the opposite bank answered.

But it was birds that dominated the soundscape, through sheer virtue of numbers. On my left, hundreds of parakeets, too small and busy to identify, gossiped incessantly amidst foliage of the exact same shade of green, while on my right, a large-billed tern called, gull-like and so evocative of the ocean. Overhead I heard a rhythmic "*Whump ... whump ... whump*" and looked up to see a muscovy duck flying towards the far end of the lake with powerful, laboured wing beats. Its flight path intersected that of another large bird, a blue-throated piping guan, gliding from one tree crown to another with a harsh rattle of its wing quills. Far away and barely audible came the ponderous "*Hum, hm hmmm ... Uh!*" of a razor-billed curassow, like a wild-haired matron clearing her throat for a stern speech. A cocoi heron replied with a raucous croak and rose majestically from its perch, sweeping to a new vantage point at the water's edge from which to spear a fish.

Turning to a fresh page in my notebook, I continued scribbling. Somewhere in the forest, a tree groaned and thudded to the ground (this happens more frequently in a rainforest than one might think) and with it came the irascible yaps of a wattled jacana. Leggy waders with outsized, delicate toes, jacanas, for some reason known only to themselves, feel compelled to complain about any and all loud noises, whether human or animal. More pleasing to my ears was the bubbling melody of a black-capped donacobius emanating from nearby marshy vegetation.

A red-eyed, Mohawk-feathered hoatzin shuffled among the branches of a large shrub ahead, wheezing softly. It reminded me of another cloudless day, on another lake. My husband and I were watching a hoatzin fly from one shore to the other, straight and true, when, inexplicably, incomprehensibly, it fell out of the sky. One moment all was well, the next it plummeted like a rotten fruit into the water. It was as though someone had decided to cut through a string that held it aloft. We rescued it and placed it carefully in a tree, unharmed though visibly shaken, and ever since I can't help but doubt the hoatzin's birdy credentials.

Pausing, my pen in mid-air, I tried to distill a moment of pure silence through the barrage of avian noise. Or, failing that, to focus on the notes of a single song. But it was impossible, like listening for your child's voice in a frenetic playground.

Wait, what was that? I held my breath. Yes, there it was again. A sharp exhalation. I knew what to look for and searched the water's surface ahead. In the shallows to the left I saw it distort and shimmer. There was a splash and a wave bulged towards me; they were chasing fish. A small, sleek head appeared ... no, two. Five! Five giant otters. And two were cubs, I could tell by the way they swam. I hastily dropped my pen and notebook, reached for my camera, and waited. The family soon spotted the boat and headed directly towards me. As the otters came closer they began to zigzag, inspecting me from all angles. One exhaled explosively and ducked under. Another propelled its upper body straight out of the water—periscoping—and I took a photo of its throat pattern. Then, letting the otters know I meant no harm, I gently paddled backwards. The important business of hunting soon distracted them and they moved past me without looking back.

Soon, high over the general hubbub, soared the piercing wails of giant otter cubs begging scraps of fish from their elders. I can't imagine more badly behaved and demanding offspring (and I've seen a few). Unlike most rainforest carnivores, giant otters are exceptionally vocal and groups do not care who hears them. This is why, for someone who has spent months observing this species, as I have, an oxbow lake without a resident giant otter family somehow lacks ... soul.

As I gazed after the otters through my binoculars, I heard, nearby, a side-necked turtle gasp in fright. I turned to look, only to find it had vanished into the tannin depths, leaving a swirl in its wake. I let the canoe drift against an overhanging shrub and waited. Five minutes later I was rewarded by a small fumbling at the edge of my vision. The turtle was hauling itself up on a partially submerged branch about ten metres away, its dark shell glistening, as though freshly varnished. Now, too, I could hear a young black caiman gulp, possibly in dismay at my presence. Another answered, and I knew their watchful mother would be nearby. I slowly scanned the dappled vegetation at the water's edge. There she was, only her head visible, a large, implacable eye, flecked with gold, monitoring my every move.

It was mid-morning now, the sun a burning weight pressing down on my shoulders. The air above the lake rustled and shimmered with gauzy insects. Thousands of dainty blue damselflies hovered low, and blood-red dragonflies darted aggressively amongst them. A welcome breeze made the water surface shiver briefly, reminding me of a horse twitching its withers to shrug off a fly. Near the bow of the canoe, rubber-lipped fish with grey snouts mouthed at bubbles and scum and tiny matter. When alarmed by an imagined threat, which seemed to happen often, they plunged downwards in unison, churning the leaf litter with a small rush of noise. My belly gurgled in sympathy. It was time for a late breakfast.

Paddling slowly back to the Station, it struck me once again how sounds travel over the water with startling clarity and are amplified as they ricochet off the wall of trees on all sides. Students laughing and chatting on a forest trail fifty metres away might as well have been in the boat with me, so near did they seem. The word 'like' featured prominently.

By the end of a Cashu day I'm usually exhausted and fall asleep the moment my head touches my sleeping bag, only to be roused the following morning by my trusty friends, the howlers. But when darkness crowds your flimsy tent, any innocent rustle quickly takes on a menacing aspect. Over breakfast one Saturday, heavy-eyed, a friend described how she'd repeatedly heard a low whistle just after midnight, exactly like the one she and her husband use as their private contact signal. She convinced herself that so-called 'uncontacted' people known as the Nomole, who live in voluntary isolation from other human societies, were nearby. Would they attack? She laughed ruefully as she spoke, but I understood how she'd felt. After all, it was common knowledge the Nomole were around, though seen only a handful of times over a period of almost five decades.

I imagine Cocha Cashu is how many places around the world used to be. How they were meant to be. Full of riotous noise, bursting at the seams with life, where the voices of wild creatures have not been interrupted and overwhelmed and silenced by our own. Now I'm back in 'civilisation', I take great comfort in knowing there are still sites like Cocha Cashu on this planet, where one can be surrounded, and deafened, by Nature.

THE MOTHER RIVER OF INDIA

Mariellen Ward

The Ganga River, lovingly referred to as Ganga Mataji, the mother river, by Hindus, speaks in many voices as she travels from the high Himalayas to the Bay of Bengal. Along the way, she slows a little to enjoy the mist-covered mountains, tulsi-filled meadows, low flying birds and grazing cattle, and provides bounty to fully one-tenth of the world's humanity in the form of water, silt, fish and the other animals drawn to her shores and depths.

As she rolls like thunder through the great expanse of the heartland of India, she collects the stories of the people on her banks. Her voice is ancient, maternal and mighty; she speaks of livelihood, duty and family; the cycles of life and death, the seasons, the inevitable, the timeless. She blesses millions, reminding them of their source and their truth.

At dusk, the lilting waters of the jewel-green Ganges River take on a more hushed tone as they flow through the holy city of Rishikesh in northern India, singing as they pass through the enchanted valley ringing with bells. She is opaque and sparkling, a beauty for the ages, decorated with flower-and-light filled offerings. Her song is joyous, full of the jubilance of youth, the rush of fresh mountain streams, the sincere chanting of pilgrims who wish her well and the excitement of the onward journey.

As darkness descended one evening in the spring of 2006, I joined pilgrims, yoga students, tourists and locals making their way to the aarti (a ceremony to honour the sacred river), held each evening on the banks of the Ganga under an enormous white statue of the Hindu god Shiva seated blissfully in lotus pose.

In Indian mythology, the Himalayan mountain range is the Abode of Shiva, the home of the Hindu god of destruction—but destruction in this sense is meant as a positive force. Shiva's energy destroys the old, unnecessary, outmoded, and unconscious; he is the transformer.

After taking off my shoes (a necessity for any sacred Hindu ritual) I decided to dive into the crowd gathering on the platform at the river's edge—though I noticed the other foreigners were standing way up on the ghats (steps), away from the action. Immediately, a family of Indian women surrounded me. Three generations of smiling women encouraged me to chant, clap and sway along to the uplifting rhythms of the devotional music. They paid as much attention to me as they did to the aarti, making sure that I felt included and knew what to do to follow along with the unfolding ritual.

Towards the end of the ceremony, the women encouraged me to buy a diya—a little boat made of leaves and filled with flowers, incense and a candle that signifies divine energy, the light of spiritual truth and the imperishable nature of the soul.

While the festival atmosphere swirled around me, I imbued my diya with hope for personal transformation. I had come to India because a river of loss had run through my life, and I had struggled with grief, despair and depression for eight years. I felt I was clinging to the bank, but the effort was wearing me out. Deciding to leave my life and go to India was like letting go of the bank and going with the flow of the river. I had no idea where it would lead me, what I would learn or how I would change. I only knew that it was going to be big.

Eight years before, on a crisp cold January morning in Toronto, I drove with my sister, Victoria, and her husband, Gary, to my mother's small apartment. She had been bedridden for a week with a terrible chest cold, but did not want to see a doctor. When we reached her building, Gary went to get a wheelchair while Victoria and I went upstairs. I knew the minute I opened the unlocked door that something was terribly wrong. I couldn't feel my mother's presence. I held out my arms in a spontaneous gesture of protection—my little sister behind me—as I realized my mother was lying in bed, dead.

In that moment a powerful force hit my stomach, chest and throat, and my back muscles locked up. I felt hit so hard, it was almost like being cleaved in two. And I knew that my mother was not in that room. I didn't know where she went, but I knew she wasn't there.

We learned later that she died in the night of heart failure. She was 67 years old.

My heart failed too, in a way. It felt as though my Mother's love had been suddenly turned off—dammed up, parching the river. I felt joyless, afraid of being "alone" on the planet without her. And her death ushered in a devastating period of loss. My fiancé left me (with an expensive wedding dress hanging in the closet). In December of 2003, my Father was diagnosed with cancer; he died three months later. As this river of loss swept through my life, I rarely went out, saw few friends, cried myself to sleep most nights. In despair, I wondered why these misfortunes had happened to me—what had I done to deserve this series of blows? And I wondered if I would be able to live through them.

To help get me out of the depression, I threw my faith into yoga. I had been going to yoga classes, on and off, and intuitively realized the healing and transformative power of this ancient art and science. I made a decision: no matter how I felt or what happened, I would go to class three times per week.

After a while, I started to feel better. I still couldn't do downward dog—there was too much tension around my broken heart—but I was starting to move and breathe again. It was like early spring. The melting ice in my veins turned to water and began to flow, giving me the energy and courage to enrol in a yoga teacher's training program. One of the teachers had recently returned from two years of yoga study in India. His teachings carried the elixir of India, which ignited in me a compulsion to live one of my dreams and go to India.

I put my things in storage, gave away my apartment, left my cat with a friend and went to India for six months.

Near the end of my trip, a friend in Delhi suggested I visit the Aurovalley Yoga Ashram near Rishikesh. At the peaceful garden ashram near the Ganga, I meditated daily, walked by the river and listened to the teachings of the founder, Swami Brahmdev, under a mango tree.

This reflective time was heaven sent. I realized that traveling in India had taught me how to surrender, relax, and go with the flow. It had reinvigorated my enthusiasm for life. "All journeys have secret destinations of which the traveler is unaware," said philosopher Martin Buber, and mine brought me one day into Rishikesh, and the evening aarti.

As I lit the diya I thought of my mother. I poured into the little boat my love for her and my feelings of intractable loss. With tears in my eyes, I sent the diya out into the current, watching as it cleared the shoal and skimmed lightly along the glossy black surface of the Ganga, a tiny retreating light in the darkness, swept along by the currents of the mighty river.

And as I watched, I allowed the magic of the ritual to transform me. I thought of the millions of people, over thousands of years, who had stood by this long, life-giving river, invoking the mother's love it symbolizes.

I felt connected—to my mother, to mother earth, to the unending cycle of life, death and rebirth that runs through the lives of every creature on this planet. Like a river. A sense of calm washed over me as I realized that my mother and I are part of this natural cycle. Her sudden death was not a tragedy, not a cause for suffering or grief, not something terrible that "happened to me." It was part of the natural pattern of life.

I felt reminded of something I always knew, but forgot. I realized we are not apart after all, my mother and I. In that moment I felt the truth of eternity open up within me. I knew that beyond the apparent reality of everyday life, something much bigger than me runs through and unites all of life. Death is an illusion.

I breathed in the primordial scene. I could feel the breath fill my lungs, and life course through me. I felt a complete sense of contentment and the warmth of quiet joy descend upon me, like the mist that drapes the distant foothills of the Himalayas. I felt love.

During the rest of my time in India I gradually and gladly embraced this shift in perception and awareness. India's gift to the world is an ancient and abiding wisdom built on the realization that reality is shaped in the mind and that the only lasting path to happiness is internal. From being the "worst thing that ever happened to me," I saw my mother's death as the catalyst for my spiritual growth and understanding.

"Suffering is a gift," Swami Bramhdev said. I understood.

ABOUT THIS BOOK

CONTRIBUTING AUTHORS

Anthony Birch

Tony Birch is the author of *Ghost River*, which won the 2016 Victorian Premier's Literary Award for Indigenous Writing and *Blood*, which was shortlisted for the Miles Franklin Award. He is also the author of *Shadowboxing*, and two short story collections, *Father's Day* and *The Promise*. In 2017 he was awarded the Patrick White Literary Prize following the release of his most recent story story collection, *Common People*. Tony is a frequent contributor to ABC local and national radio and a regular guest at writers' festivals. He lives in Melbourne and is a Senior Research Fellow at Victoria University.

Rob Carney

Rob Carney grew up in the Pacific Northwest but has lived for the last twenty-one years in Salt Lake City, Utah. He is the author of five books of poems, most recently *The Book of Sharks* (Black Lawrence Press 2018) and *88 Maps* (Lost Horse Press 2015), which was named a finalist for the Washington State Book Award. In 2014 he received the Robinson Jeffers/Tor House Foundation Award for Poetry. His work has appeared in *Cave Wall, Poecology, The American Journal of Poetry*, and many others, as well as the *Norton anthology Flash Fiction Forward* (2006). He is a Professor of English at Utah Valley University and writes a regular feature called 'Old Roads, New Stories' for *Terrain: A Journal of the Built and Natural Environments*.

Kathleen Dean Moore

Kathleen Dean Moore, Ph.D., is a philosopher and writer, best known for award-winning books about our cultural and spiritual relation to wet, wild places. Among them are *Riverwalking, Holdfast, Pine Island Paradox,* and *Wild Comfort*. Until recently Distinguished Professor of Environmental Ethics at Oregon State University, Moore's love for the reeling world has led her to a new life of climate writing and activism. Her most recent book, *Great Tide Rising: Toward Clarity and Moral Courage in a Time of Planetary Change,* follows the pivotal *Moral Ground: Ethical Action for a Planet in Peril*, testimony from the world's moral leaders about our obligations to the future. Moore's environmental writing returns to the wild-weather coast in her newest book, *The Piano Tide*, "a savagely funny and deeply insightful" novel about a small town's struggle to defend its fresh water. Her work has won the Pacific Northwest Bookseller's Association Award, the Oregon Book Award, the WILLA Award for Contemporary

Fiction, and the Sigurd Olson Nature Writing Award. She writes from Corvallis, Oregon and from a small cabin where two creeks and a bear trail meet a tidal cove in Alaska.

Louise Duff

Louise Duff has been working to engage communities in nature conservation since 1988. She has a focus on wetland and shorebird conservation under the framework of the Ramsar Convention. Her professional role involves engaging communities in practical conservation of wetland, catchments and coasts, managing Conservation Volunteers Australia's Revive Our Wetlands program. Her previous roles include Regional Manager for Wetlandcare Australia and Chief Executive Officer for Hunter Wetlands Centre. Louise was appointed the Oceania Representative to the World Wetland Network in 2011 and became the Chair in 2016. She attended Ramsar COP 11 and 12, working with the WWN committee to facilitate the effective participation of NGOs.

Wes Ferguson

American writer and journalist Wes Ferguson is the author of two nonfiction books, *The Blanco River* and *Running the River: Secrets of the Sabine*, both published by Texas A&M University Press. A former ski instructor for Mount Hotham in the Victorian Alps, Ferguson lives in Austin, Texas, with his wife, Laura. He is a regular contributor for magazines in the United States and is working on his third book.

Let the River Run is excerpted from The Blanco River, by Wes Ferguson (Texas A&M University Press , 2017).

Jessica Groenendijk

Jessica Groenendijk is a Dutch biologist and nature writer, based in Peru. Her work in conservation has taken her from monitoring the charismatic and irrepressible giant otter in the Amazon rainforest to helping to protect endangered black rhinos in Zambia. She is currently the Communications Coordinator of the Cocha Cashu Biological Station in Manu National Park, for San Diego Zoo Global. Jessica has been published in BBC Wildlife Magazine, Africa Geographic, Earth Island Journal, The Island Review, Sevenseas, and Zoomorphic, amongst others, and is the co-author of All Things Breathe Alike. Her latest book, on giant otters and their conservation, will be published in February 2019. Read Jessica's work at jessicagroenendijk.com.

A version of Deafened by Nature was originally published as Into The Presence of Still Water by The Island Review (July 28, 2017).

Lisa Knopp

Lisa Knopp is the author of six books of creative nonfiction. Her most recent, Bread: A Memoir of Hunger, is about eating disorders and disordered eating among older women. Both *Bread* and *What the River Carries: Encounters with the Mississippi, Missouri, and Platte* won Nebraska Book Awards. Knopp's essays have appeared in numerous literary journals including *Georgia Review, Missouri Review, Michigan Review, Gettysburg Review, Crab Orchard Review, Connecticut Review, Iowa Review, Shenandoah, Creative Nonfiction, Prairie Schooner,* and *Seneca Review.* Her current project is *Like Salt or Love: Essays on Leaving Home.* Knopp is a Professor of English at the University of Nebraska-Omaha, where she teaches courses in creative nonfiction. She lives in Lincoln, Nebraska. Read Lisa's work at lisaknopp.com

Catfish Bend was originally published in *Natural Bridge* (University of Missouri-St. Louis, Fall 2011).

It was republished in *What the River Carries: Encounters with the Mississippi, Missouri, and Platte* (University of Missouri Press 2012).

Rebecca Lawton

Rebecca Lawton is a writer, fluvial geologist, and former Colorado River guide who has published in *Aeon, Brevity, Hakai, Orion, Shenandoah, Sierra, THEMA, Undark,* and many other journals. She is the author and co-author of seven books, including the *San Francisco Chronicle* Bay Area Bestseller *Reading Water: Lessons from the River.* Her writing honors include a Fulbright Visiting Research Chair, the Ellen Meloy Award for Desert Writers, a WILLA for original softcover fiction, the Waterston Desert Writing Prize, three Pushcart nominations, a Best American Science and Nature

Writing nomination, and residencies at Hedgebrook, The Island Institute, and Playa.

  Prodigal River was first published in *Reading Water: Lessons from the River* (Capital Books, 2002).

Karen Lloyd

Karen Lloyd is a writer of creative non-fiction and poetry based in Kendal, Cumbria. Her first book, *The Gathering Tide; A Journey Around the Edgelands of Morecambe Bay* contains writing on land, landscape and memory. It won Eric Robson's Striding Edge Productions Prize for Place and was runner up at The Lakeland Book of the Year Awards 2016. Her most recent book is *The Blackbird Diaries*, a closely observed journal documenting the wildlife in her South Lakeland garden and further afield, including Scotland's Solway coast and the Hebridean islands of Mull and Staffa. Karen graduated with distinction from the M.Litt at Stirling University. She writes for *The Guardian Country Diary, BBC Countryfile Magazine*, The Royal Geographic Society website, *Discovering Britain* and a number of other journals. She is a member of Kendal's Brewery Poets and is currently undertaking a Ph.D. at Lancaster University, where her research project is a literary exploration of species that are doing well against a backdrop of wider loss.